Keeping Christmas

Keeping Christmas

25 Advent Reflections
on
A Christmas Carol

Allison Pittman

BakerBooks

a division of Baker Publishing Group
Grand Rapids, Michigan

Published by Baker Books
a division of Baker Publishing Group
PO Box 6287, Grand Rapids, MI 49516-6287
www.bakerbooks.com

Printed in the United States of America

Library of Congress Cataloging-in-Publication Data
Names: Pittman, Allison, author.
Title: Keeping Christmas : 25 advent reflections on a Christmas
    carol / Allison Pittman.
Description: Grand Rapids, Michigan : Baker Books, 2020.
Identifiers: LCCN 2020007088 | ISBN 9781540900067 (hardcover)
Subjects: LCSH: Dickens, Charles, 1812–1870. Christmas
    carol. | Dickens, Charles, 1812–1870.—Adaptations. |
    Advent—Meditations.
Classification: LCC PR4572.I885 P57 2020 | DDC 823/.8—dc23
LC record available at https://lccn.loc.gov/2020007088

Unless otherwise indicated, Scripture quotations are from the Holy Bible, New International Version®. NIV®. Copyright © 1973, 1978, 1984, 2011 by Biblica, Inc.™ Used by permission of Zondervan. All rights reserved worldwide. www.zondervan.com. The "NIV" and "New International Version" are trademarks registered in the United States Patent and Trademark Office by Biblica, Inc.™

Scripture quotations labeled ESV are from The Holy Bible, English Standard Version® (ESV®), copyright © 2001 by Crossway, a publishing ministry of Good News Publishers. Used by permission. All rights reserved. ESV Text Edition: 2016

Scripture quotations labeled KJV are from the King James Version of the Bible.

A Christmas Carol quotations and illustrations are from the original work: Charles Dickens, *A Christmas Carol in Prose, Being a Ghost Story of Christmas*, illustrated by John Leech (London: Chapman & Hall, 1843), https://www.gutenberg.org/files/46/46-h/46 -h.htm. Subtle changes to the text have been made since 1843.

The author is represented by William K. Jensen Literary Agency.

20 21 22 23 24 25 26   7 6 5 4 3 2 1

Contents

Contents

Author's Note

ear Reader,

    Charles Dickens opens his novella *A Christmas Carol* with this:

> I have endeavoured in this Ghostly little book, to raise the Ghost of an Idea, which shall not put my readers out of humour with themselves, with each other, with the season, or with me. May it haunt their houses pleasantly, and no one wish to lay it.
>
> Their faithful Friend and Servant,
C. D.

I humbly offer the same plea.

As a reader, scholar, teacher, and writer, I have always had a deep-rooted fascination with this particular work. I've seen nearly every version ever filmed, from the silent movie available on YouTube to the iconic Lifetime adaptation starring the inimitable Susan Lucci. The arc of the story never changes. Ebenezer Scrooge, no matter the actor who hosts the character, comes off as a miserable person. Mean, greedy, abrasive—and lonely. There are circumstances as to why he (or she, e.g., Tori Spelling) feels that way. And three supernatural beings guide us through the past, the present, and the future. Watch *Scrooged*,

Scrooge, or *Scrooge!* They all have it. As does *A Christmas Carol*, *A Carol Christmas*, or *An American Christmas Carol*. Scrooge has been embodied by a former Miss America (Vanessa Williams) and a former Fonzie (Henry Winkler). The tale has been animated by pen and ink, augmented by CGI, and cast with Muppets in which a birdish Gonzo plays the role of Dickens himself. No matter what liberties are taken with the story (a dance number in hell, two Marley brothers to capture a Bob Marley moment), the end is the same. All of the Scrooges confront their sins, repent, and go on to live kinder, more generous lives.

It takes a reading of the original text, however, to capture the true, spiritual essence of Scrooge's transformation. A close—very close—reading reveals his visits to be more than simple encounters with supernatural beings; they are confrontations with Christ—the One in whose name we celebrate this season. Scrooge doesn't just become a better man, he becomes a new man. So, just as Scrooge relies on the Spirits to guide him on this pilgrimage of self-awareness, I beg the opportunity to offer myself to guide you through the text of this beloved Christmas classic. Maybe, like me, you've read the original a dozen times and will—again, like me—see something in a new light. Perhaps you've watched some film adaptation every Christmas of your life, but you haven't delved into the text. If that's the case, I invite you to grab a copy to read for yourself. I promise the dense prose that may have seemed intimidating in the past will come to life. It did for me, in the same paragraphs and pages I thought I knew by heart. The difference being, I gave the story over to my heart, looking past Scrooge's obvious, outside transformation to find the profound inner change that brings it about. He is not, with all compliments to Dr. Seuss's Grinch, a creature whose heart merely grows. He is a man whose heart is transplanted.

Full disclosure: I am not a theologian or any kind of Dickensian scholar. I'm an English teacher who has devoted a lifetime to helping students wrangle with symbolism and metaphor. And I'm a writer who strives to bring fictitious souls to Christ within every work. For us, as we travel this little book together, I hope to bring the best of both of my worlds—to enlighten, to lead, and to share bits and pieces of my own story.

Throughout my study for this work, I clung to the promise found in 2 Corinthians 5:17–19: "Therefore, if anyone is in Christ, the new creation has come: The old has gone, the new is here! All this is from God, who reconciled us to himself through Christ and gave us the ministry of reconciliation: that God was reconciling the world to himself in Christ, not counting people's sins against them. And he has committed to us the message of reconciliation."

I see Dickens's tale as a message of reconciliation as well as an illustration of the life we ought to live once reconciled to Christ. It's not only a journey through the past, present, and future but also a journey from death to life. Not just a reclamation but a rebirth.

The season of Advent is itself a journey: twenty-four days to mark the moment when Jesus Christ came to transform the world. But it is so much more than just a Christmas countdown; it's a time when we can celebrate our own transformational experience. The long winter nights of Advent are meant to be a time of contemplation, reflection, anticipation. The story of Scrooge happens over the course of one of those nights—a matter of hours—a time of confrontation, repentance, and salvation.

And so, to paraphrase:

I have endeavored with this little book to raise up the eternal truths, which shall not raise the ire of Dickensian scholars, theologians, Christmas fanatics, or classic film buffs. May it haunt your hearts pleasantly.

A faithful Friend and Servant of Christ,

A. P.

1

Dead, to Begin With

arley was dead: to begin with. There is no doubt whatever about that."

These days, with the Christmas season so full of white twinkle lights and red silk ribbons adorning unnaturally green trees, it's hard to reconcile such a bleak, grave statement with the story so synonymous with the holiday. The register of his burial was signed by the clergyman, the clerk, the undertaker, and the chief mourner. In other words, he was dead, dead, dead, dead.

"Old Marley was as dead as a door-nail."

Marley was so dead . . .

(How dead was he?)

Deader than a coffin nail.

Deader than a two-a-penny nail.

Dead enough to earn the phrase that we all still use to drive a point home like a hammer on a nail head.

Not deader than a doornail, mind you. Because once you're a doornail, well, you aren't going to get much deader.

But dead.

Gone.

Undertaken and buried.

Merry Christmas.

God begins his Christmas story in much the same way.

"But . . . but!" thousands of Sunday school teachers and Nativity scene collectors and pseudosecular celebrators decry. Christmas is the "Infant Holy," "Away in the Manger," the "Silent Night, Holy Night" where unto us a child is born. Pregnant Mary. Stalwart Joseph. Infant Jesus. Cattle lowing, donkeys looking on, sheep following shepherds following a star. Christmas is life.

All true. But the life of Christmas, like all life as it cycles through God's creation, begins with death. We cannot sing "O, Little Town of Bethlehem" without also pondering the lyrics of "Mary, Did You Know?" Yes, we know the sweet story of the swaddled child, but we also know the story of that same child, grown and crucified. We know those chubby hands will be pierced; the downy head will someday wear a crown of thorns. The shepherds left their fields to behold a perfect lamb born for slaughter. Quite the sobering shadow on your Nativity scene.

The timeline of the Scriptures holds a sharp divide. Old Testament. New Testament. The opening chapters of the Gospels are resplendent with life. With beginnings. John takes us to the birth of the universe, where there was nothing but the Word. Mark promises to tell a story about the Good News. Luke sets out to write an orderly account for you, most excellent Theophilus. Matthew starts with the family tree: a record of the genealogy of Jesus Christ, the son of David, the son of Abraham. Any of these texts would be perfect for the voice-over narration in the church Christmas program. (Especially John, if you want to add a certain gravitas to the shepherds in the field.) All those elements of the Nativity are so achingly familiar, it's easy to forget what came just before.

The nothingness.

The silence.

Before that, in the waning verses of the last of the Old Testament prophets, Malachi speaks a dire warning: "'Surely the day is coming; it will burn like a furnace. All the arrogant and every evildoer will be stubble, and the day that is coming will set them on fire,' says the LORD Almighty" (Mal. 4:1).

And after that, silence. Malachi dies, and the tongues of God's prophets fall still for four hundred years.

Nothing spoken to the clergymen.

Nothing recorded by the clerks.

Mute, like a doornail.

That's not to say that God didn't speak during that time. I'm sure he communicated as he always has, whispering directly to the hearts of righteous people. Clearing paths so the wise might follow. Gentle rebukes of conscience in the face of sin. Still, four centuries go by without anything to pass the muster of recorded Scripture. Nothing for the masses—no encouragement, no warnings. Prophecy nailed shut until the time was right to wrench it open and start a New Testament for humankind.

Too many film adaptations of *A Christmas Carol* skip over the death of Marley. They like to open with the snow-strewn Victorian avenue, carolers plowing through the third verse of "Good King Wenceslas," men tipping top hats, delicacies displayed in candlelit windows. A book shop. Sweet shop. Tailors and haberdashers. The Hallmark Entertainment production (from the days when Hallmark took their Christmas programming a little more seriously) starring Patrick Stewart, however, opens with a black, horse-drawn hearse. Marley's casket in a grave surrounded by snow-cold ground. Scriptures about life being fleeting, like a flower. Sown in misery. Later, the sound of a scratching quill, the book signed to certify Marley's eternal state.

Melodramatic? Yes. Perfectly so.

Marley was dead. Later, readers learn he's been dead seven years. A perfected number of years, to be exact. He died on the eve of Christmas. He's been dead long enough for the forces of nature to erase his name from the sign hanging outside of his place of business. Dickens implies this same time of silence, for the story picks up with the single living soul who stood as chief mourner at the officiation of Marley's death. The reader must be completely, fully accepting that the time of Marley is over, that his voice is removed from all natural sound.

Marley is dead.

Scrooge, on the other hand, is very much alive.

Well, mostly.

2

Covetous Old Sinner

benezer Scrooge.

Like all of Charles Dickens's most memorable characters, the pronouncing of his name brings the speaker's lips into a mirthful twist. It is a combination of ancient, established weight and authorial whimsy. Ebenezer, meaning "stone of help," references a stone placed by the prophet Samuel after God saved the Israelites from being destroyed by the Philistines (1 Sam. 7:10–12). And Scrooge, a name that—according to the film *The Man Who Invented Christmas*—Dickens came up with after a night of pacing the floor making noises to himself. The two names come together to create this man who, perhaps unlike any other fictional character ever penned, is simultaneously hated and pitied. We the readers root for Scrooge as much as we despise him. He is a villain without any real enemy. An antihero with no cause beyond himself.

And, when he first appears upon the page, he is—like his best and only true friend, Jacob Marley—dead. Or he may as well be.

"Sometimes people new to the business called Scrooge, Scrooge, and sometimes Marley, but he answered to both names. It was all the same to him."

Scrooge has not, of course, achieved doornail status. Outwardly he is very much alive, as filmmakers tend to portray him as a man full of vitality, storming through the Victorian streets, his walking stick attacking the ice at each step. His voice, when he bursts into his office, is booming and strident (although the novel describes it as shrewd and grating). He is a man of vigor; death itself—of any natural cause—seems a possibility as distant as spring, and anybody who wishes his demise faces decades of disappointment.

Dickens captures this paradox in his introduction of the "tight-fisted, hand at the grindstone, Scrooge!" First, there are the verbs: "a squeezing, wrenching, grasping, scraping, clutching covetous old sinner!" His actions may not be admirable, but he is active. And if Ebenezer denotes a man of stone, such is Scrooge: "hard and sharp as flint, from which no steel had ever struck out generous fire."

There is a lifeless chill to the man as well. "A frosty rime was on his head, and on his eyebrows, and his wiry chin." Now, having a head of white hair and a white beard doesn't automatically carry a feeling of death. Other icons of the Christmas season (you know who you are) might fit the same description. But Scrooge emits no jolly holiday spirit. In fact, quite the opposite. "He carried his own low temperature always about with him; he iced his office in the dog-days, and didn't thaw it one degree at Christmas."

All of this puts him in the perfect place for transformation.

Death to life.

Where Dickens points out that Scrooge is a "covetous old sinner," the apostle Paul makes it a point to say that we are all as such: "You were dead in your transgressions and sins" (Eph. 2:1). He goes on to say, "God, who is rich in mercy, made us alive with Christ even when we were dead in transgressions" (vv. 4–5).

Scrooge squeezes and wrenches and grasps, even as he's blue-lipped and dead.

Beggars avoid him; children fear him. "Even the blind men's dogs . . . would tug their owners into doorways and up courts."

And the kicker? That's exactly how Scrooged liked it, evidence of just how powerful his transformation will be.

His story begins at the peak of his season of Advent. Only, he hasn't been preparing himself. He's been prepared. He's like that perfect Christmas cookie, crisped around the edges but soft in the middle. He just doesn't know about his own softness.

"External heat and cold had little influence on Scrooge. No warmth could warm, no wintry weather chill him." In other words, he was impervious to the influences of the world. He is poised between heartbeats. He'll either have another—life. Or he won't—death. Ultimately that choice will be his, but the opportunity to make that choice comes to Scrooge in the same way it comes to all of us.

We'll see, over the course of the story, that Scrooge does nothing good. As far as we know, he never has done anything good. Chances are, if not for the supernatural intervention in his path, he never will do anything good. And without Christ, without the Savior we celebrate this season, the same could be said for all of us.

Too often, we stride through life with our hard edges exposed. We speak sharp words to drown out our insecurities. We ignore opportunities for good deeds because such might cut into our plans. Look around and see how many people are out-n-about this season, heads bent, brows furrowed, faces pinched. Think about how many human interactions we decline, simply because to engage might mean there might not be . . . enough. Enough time, enough money, enough attention—for ourselves.

But God is merciful.

He can lift us up by those hard edges and speak straight into our soft center.

Left to his own devices, Scrooge might have lived the rest of his days secret and self-contained and solitary as an oyster. He would continue to edge his way along the crowded paths of life, warning all human sympathy to keep its distance. But he is not left to his own devices.

And they're waiting for him in his very own counting house. The one he used to share with Jacob Marley. But then, remember? Marley's dead. And when Scrooge opens the door, even though it's cold enough to see the steam of his breath within the room, that breath means one thing.

His heart is still beating.

3

Good Afternoon, Gentlemen!

And now abideth faith, hope, charity, these three; but the greatest of these is charity.

1 Corinthians 13:13 KJV

nce upon a time—of all the good days in the year, on Christmas Eve—old Scrooge sat busy in his counting-house."

It might be a cozy scene, dark and foggy, with Scrooge in the front room and his clerk, the mild Bob Cratchit, toiling away in the smaller room beyond. But coziness requires a fire, bits of conversation, maybe a cup of tea. Instead we have fog rolling in through the keyholes and fingers so stiffened with cold they can barely function. Scrooge keeps the door to Cratchit's alcove open, not so they can exchange cheerful quips of conversation but so he can keep an eye on his clerk, lest the poor man try to warm his office with an additional shovelful of coal.

And it's Christmas Eve.

We all know Christmas Eve as that night of unbearable anticipation. The night children nestle with sugary dreams. It's when courageous reindeer burst through the fog, red noses blazing. Brave nutcracker soldiers come to life. Grinchy plans go awry.

History gives us three Eves of Christ: the night before he is born, the night before he is crucified, and the night before he rises. Three befores, three afters. A birth, a death, a resurrection. Three times the world is irreversibly changed.

On one of those eves, Jesus rightfully predicts that Peter will deny him three times. Peter protests, "Even if I have to die with you, I will never disown you" (Matt. 26:35). But, of course, he does.

So too in this opening scene, Scrooge passes up three opportunities to acknowledge Christmas.

First, he is greeted by his affable nephew, Fred, who generously invites Scrooge to spend Christmas with him and his family. (We get the impression that this is an annual occurrence, both the invitation and the refusal.) This is where Scrooge utters his first iconic "Humbug!"

Next, his offices are visited by the gentlemen soliciting businesses for charitable donations: "Some slight provision for the Poor and destitute, who suffer greatly . . ."

These poor guys have no idea what they're getting into, asking Ebenezer Scrooge to donate to the "hundreds of thousands . . . in want of common comforts." Perhaps Marley was a softer touch back in the day, but Marley's been gone these seven years. Not only does Scrooge offer "Nothing!"; his solution to poverty in London is to send the poor to prisons and workhouses. When one of the gentlemen says that many would rather die than go to such places, Scrooge delivers his most hate-filled denial of Christmas: "'If they would rather die,' said Scrooge, 'they had better do it, and decrease the surplus population.'"

The line that follows, though, speaks to his denial. He says, after being confronted with the plight of the poor in his city, "Besides— excuse me—I don't know that."

To which the gentleman says, "But you might know it."

And Scrooge replies, "It's not my business. It's enough for a man to understand his own business, and not to interfere with other people's. Mine occupies me constantly."

So too does the apostle Peter, when a servant girl confronts him, observes him, looks at him closely, and says she saw him with Jesus of Nazareth. Peter says, "I don't know . . . what you're talking about" (Mark 14:68). He dismisses her just as Scrooge dismisses Fred and the gentlemen. Peter denies knowing Christ; Scrooge denies knowing the means to be Christlike.

Peter, all wound up in panic and guilt and fear, escalated the tone of his third response.

A little later some of the other bystanders confronted Peter and said, "Surely you are one of them, for you are a Galilean." He began to call down curses on himself and swore to them, "I don't know this man you're talking about." Immediately the rooster crowed a second time, and Jesus's words flashed through Peter's mind: "Before the rooster crows twice you will disown me three times." Peter broke down and wept (see vv. 70–72).

Scrooge, too, gets a little overheated. When an innocent boy stands at the door to offer a sweet Christmas carol, Scrooge charges out, brandishing a ruler like a whip, sending the offending songsters to scatter in the snow. Their song is Scrooge's cock-crow. But where Peter's reaction is swift—he breaks down, weeping—well, Scrooge isn't quite there yet.

He says to his long-suffering clerk, Bob Cratchit:

"You'll want all day to-morrow, I suppose?"

"If quite convenient, sir."

"It's not convenient," said Scrooge, "and it's not fair. If I was to stop half-a-crown for it, you'd think yourself ill used, I'll be bound?"

The clerk smiled faintly.

Look there for a moment. "The clerk smiled faintly." Cratchit has just observed this man, his boss, insulting the lovable Fred, speaking a death wish upon the poor, and threatening violence to a child singing a blessing to Merry Gentlemen. And yet, Cratchit smiles, because he knows—deep down—that Scrooge will relent.

Jesus always knew what Peter would become to him. To his followers and his church. Even before those pesky moments of denial, Jesus said to him, "And I tell you, you are Peter, and on this rock I will build my church, and the gates of hell shall not prevail against it" (Matt. 16:18).

Can you even imagine how wonderful life would be—how reassuringly simple and stress-free—if we could have such a conversation with Jesus? If he could look us in the eye and say, "This is who you are, and THIS is who you will be." But even in those moments when we feel so far, far away from his voice, when we're mired in the consequences of decisions we made in our Eve of Denial—he sees us. More importantly, he allows us the opportunity to see him. To know him. Hebrews 10:36 speaks of the promise we receive when we come out of the dark and step into the life he has been planning for us all along.

In the final pages of *A Christmas Carol*, Ebenezer ("stone of help") will become the one of whom it was always said, "He knew how to keep Christmas well, if any man alive possessed the knowledge." He will come to accept Christmas, to practice Christmas, to live Christmas—this same man who, hours before, denied any connection with the holiday and lived without any evidence of connection to the One for whom the holiday is named.

So there's the eve, the cock-crow, and the dawn.

Right now, for Scrooge, night is still falling.

4

Air Filled with Phantoms

t's a delightfully creepy moment played large in every adaptation: the cinematic overlay of Jacob Marley's face, straight from the grave, in place of Scrooge's humble door knocker. A wretched rag holds tight his unhinged jaw. Sometimes Marley greets with a ghostly "Mwa-haha-haaa." Other times, he's left as a silent trick of the eye. In the novel, Scrooge sees him as he'd seen him in life, with ghostly spectacles turned up on his ghostly forehead and a mysterious breeze ruffling his hair. His eyes wide and staring; a face beyond the specter's control.

What follows is textbook screenplay for every ghost and horror story ever produced: Scrooge hears noises; Scrooge ignores noises. Bells ring, boards creak, scuttles scuttle. He keeps the house dark because it's cheaper. (We in the audience scream, "Turn on a light!") He makes his way around the rooms, looking under furniture and behind doors. He's startled by a suspiciously hanging dressing gown but, satisfied in his solitude, settles down only to hear—

The chains.

Marley appears. Rather, the ghost of Marley appears. He is shackled by all that enslaved him in life—money, business, success.

The ghost of a dead, rich man.

In chapter 16 of the Gospel of Luke, Jesus tells his own story of a dead rich man, splendidly clothed in purple and fine linen, who lived each day in luxury (v. 19). The rich man remains unnamed throughout the parable, but there is a poor man, Lazarus, who would lay at the gate, longing for scraps from the rich man's table. At some point, both men die. Lazarus is carried away to sit beside Abraham at a heavenly banquet. When the rich man dies, he is buried and sent to a place of torment. Fiery hellish flames. As an added torture, he can see that poor wretch Lazarus. He shouts to father Abraham, "Have pity on me and send Lazarus to dip the tip of his finger in water and cool my tongue, because I am in agony in this fire" (v. 24).

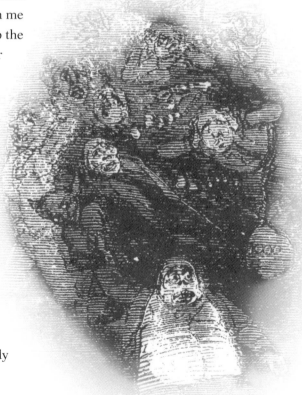

This particular chapter from Luke's Gospel never gets to be the narration of a church's Christmas pageant. It doesn't exactly lend itself to dressing children in adorable shepherd costumes and having the excitement of a live donkey on stage. Nobody wants to see their child dressed as ragged Lazarus with a family pet licking pepperoni sores. A shame, because its lesson plays a huge part in what we celebrate at Christmas, when almost everyone is inclined to reach a little deeper into their pockets and give to all the organizations that help the Lazaruses at our gates. This parable, like *A Christmas Carol*, impresses the godliness of lifelong generosity. The sharing of wealth. The importance of giving while you're alive. While you can. Otherwise, you end up a rich man burning in hell, asking for a bit of water to be touched to your tongue only to hear, "Son, remember that in your lifetime you received your good things, while Lazarus received bad things, but now he is comforted here and you are in agony" (v. 25).

Dickens banishes the wealthy deceased to the bitter-cold streets of London. Marley takes Scrooge to look out his own window where the air is thick with phantoms, each wearing the shackles of their life's work: fine clothes and money boxes. At least one was well known to Scrooge, remembered as a successful man of business. Just like Marley. Just like Scrooge. In this moment, too, we see another point in which the dead and the living merge—almost. The phantom sees a woman seeking shelter in a doorway. Dying, probably. She is certainly cold, hungry, and clutching an infant who—if she does die—will soon suffer the same fate.

And the phantom can do nothing to help her. Unlike the rich man in Jesus's parable, this dead man knows better than to seek his own comfort. What he longs for is to comfort her. His anguish—which he shares with all his fellow ghosts—is his helplessness.

"The misery with them all was, clearly, that they sought to interfere, for good, in human matters, and had lost the power forever."

To think, an hour before, Scrooge walked right past her.

But we've all had those moments, haven't we? Those of us who live in urban areas know what it's like to stride past the homeless or to lock our car doors where panhandlers are working the intersections. Raise your hand if you've ever claimed not to have cash when you do have cash, but not in bills small enough to drop in a cup. All of us have, at one time or another, walked right past a hungry person without offering a crumb, even though our consciences might prick with every step. Those people, living in the fringes of our comfortable lives, can haunt us. Those missed opportunities for generosity can follow us around and impact us in two ways. They can pile, one on top of the other, wrapping lock-box hearts in chains. Or, with a bit of prompting, we can try to do more—do better, do something—next time.

Perhaps watching Scrooge step over the woman in his doorway is what spurred Jacob Marley to visit his old pal. Unlike other bogus Christmas angel stories, there's no reward for Marley if or when Scrooge has a change of heart. He's not going to get Wonderful Life Wings, or any other kind of Good Place Promotion. His is merely a mission of good, to warn a friend from living a life of the same mistakes. To give Scrooge the chance no one gave him.

The rich man in the parable pleads for such an ambassador. He implores Abraham to send Lazarus to his five brothers, whom we can assume are equally wealthy, to warn them to embark immediately on a life of charity. But Abraham will not be swayed, saying that the rich brothers can read the writings of Moses and the prophets and figure it out for themselves.

The rich man begs, "No, father Abraham, . . . but if someone from the dead goes to them, they will repent" (v. 30).

But Abraham says, "If they do not listen to Moses and the Prophets, they will not be convinced even if someone rises from the dead" (v. 31).

I would call it a pretty safe assumption that more people have watched some version of *A Christmas Carol* than have read the parable of the rich man and Lazarus. The universality of Christ's message in the parable is clear: the rich man is condemned because of his treatment of the poor. Dickens holds true to Jesus's claim in this— Marley is not risen from the dead. He is dead. Remember? Dead. As. A. Doornail. But, Scrooge will be persuaded by the personae of one who *has* risen from the dead.

The three Spirits of Christmas.

And the first is due when the bell tolls one.

Sleep tight!

5

Evergreen and Summer Flowers
Christ in Christmas Past

hree paintings—
>*Madonna and Child*, Duccio di Buoninsegna.
>*Madonna Enthroned*, Giotto di Bondone.

Madonna with Child (Lippina), Filippo Lippi.

All have this one thing in common: ugly babies. As much as we want to insist that all babies are beautiful, honesty compels us to admit that a certain percentage of them look like shriveled, cranky-faced old men. Curl them up in a pea pod, stick 'em in a pumpkin, roll them in a Santa hat—nothing can guarantee cuteness in a newborn. Your Pinterest boards are full of lies.

Pre-Reformation and Byzantine Era artists faced a dilemma creating the Christ child on canvas. Religious paintings were a part of religious instruction, icons that required accurate symbology to teach the truth of Scripture to illiterate masses. And so, whatever roly-poly cuteness we expect in a baby had to give way to an effort to capture the expression of a tiny human who just happens to be the God of all creation. Thus an old-man face superimposed onto a little body, leaving us with something like—in Buoninsegna's case especially—the Virgin Mary with a tiny insurance agent on her lap.

Disconcerting.

Colossians 2:8–9 says it quite clearly: "See to it that no one takes you captive through hollow and deceptive philosophy, which depends on human tradition and the elemental spiritual forces of this world rather than on Christ. For in Christ all the fullness of the Deity lives in bodily form."

Paul knew that people would look to any means to be "good" and find fulfillment in life other than in Christ. If you think about it, feeding the hungry and helping the poor are basic principles of *this* world, and doing so does make you a better human being in this world. Scrooge might learn valuable lessons in how to be a human from the talking ghost and floating phantoms, but neither can secure his eternity. For that, he needs to hear from Christ himself. Like the brothers of the rich man in the parable, however, he's not likely to spend his time searching the Scriptures. Jacob Marley knows this about him. Dickens knows this about his audience. If they did, he wouldn't have been writing to a city where the hungry and poor lay dying in prisons, workhouses, and streets.

The author was faced with the same dilemma that plagued his predecessors in the art world: how to depict the simultaneous humanity and deity of Christ.

This is what he came up with:

> It was a strange figure—like a child: yet not so like a child as like an old man, viewed through some supernatural medium, which gave him the appearance of having receded from the view, and being diminished to a child's proportions. Its hair, which hung about its neck and down

its back, was white as if with age; and yet the face had not a wrinkle in it, and the tenderest bloom was on the skin. The arms were very long and muscular; the hands the same, as if its hold were of uncommon strength. Its legs and feet, most delicately formed, were, like those upper members, bare. It wore a tunic of the purest white, and round its waist was bound a lustrous belt, the sheen of which was beautiful. It held a branch of fresh green holly in its hand; and, in singular contradiction of that wintry emblem, had its dress trimmed with summer flowers. But the strangest thing about it was, that from the crown of its head there sprung a clear jet of light, by which all this was visible; and which was doubtless the occasion of its using, in its duller moments, a great extinguisher for a cap, which it now held under its arm.

Hollywood never gets this character right. The Spirit of Christmas Past has been played by a woman, a sprightly old gent, an actual child, an animated flame. Always, there is a missing element. A personal favorite is the effort made by Jim Henson in *The Muppet Christmas Carol*, in which a moon-faced creature, with delicate lines etched into the felt of its face, was filmed underwater, giving it a floaty, glow-y effect. But then, that incarnation fails to incorporate the clear jet of light, which is crucial.

Because Jesus is the Light.

The contradictory elements of age and infancy are clear in the Spirit. So too does Dickens present the mortality and immortality of Christ. The Spirit holds a branch of fresh green holly—just one of the many symbols Christians snuck away from the pagans to give a fresh coat of meaning. Dickens's audience would be familiar with the old song, "The Holly and the Ivy," which inextricably links the plant to the life and death of Jesus. The holly leaf is eternally green, its berries as red as the droplets of blood beneath the Savior's crown of thorns; its leaves sharp enough to be the crown itself. With this, however, Dickens pairs a dress trimmed with summer flowers, an unmistakable nod to the finite time Jesus will spend in his earthly body. As Psalm 103:15 states, "The life of mortals is like grass, they flourish like a flower of the field; the wind blows over it and it is gone."

Jesus, we know, will bloom and die. And rise again, his eternal state uninterrupted.

What follows in the story is a rather bizarre paragraph, in which the Ghost of Christmas Past—under the power of the flashing light of its belt—seems to morph in and out of sight, in and out of form, with legs and arms multiplying and disappearing, melting away and then zapping back into its recognizable self. Again, in that sense, the essence of Christ is so impossible to capture. Scripture calls him a lamb, a light, the Word. Wholly immortal, he took on a season of mortality. He is the Creator of the universe who walked among his creation. He is ever-loving but was sometimes angry. He holds all the answers but would teach through questions. He is the only God who lived, and the only God who died, and the only God to live again. The only God who lives still. He changed the world without raising a flag or a weapon.

Death, Life, Man, God, Mortal, Eternal.

And, he sees us. He knows all our dark corners. All our memories. All our hurts. For some, such a thought is comforting. Hopeful.

For Scrooge? Terrifying. Scarier than Byzantine baby Jesus.

But what scares Scrooge the most is the light. The Light, from which he has fought so long to hide. It's about to shine brightly now, through the night. Through his life. One touch of the Spirit's hand, and—

Go.

6

Home, Dear Brother!

few snapshot memories of my childhood Christmases and schooling:

Learning to sing "Jingle Bells" in multiple languages. Wait, no. Not languages, but accents and dialects that, thinking about it now, were incredibly culturally insensitive.

Choosing an art project to make as a Christmas gift for my parents. One of the choices was an ashtray. An ashtray. Because who wouldn't want to encourage their parents' dangerous habit?

Making endless red-and-green construction-paper chains; cutting a storm's worth of snowflakes (no two alike); linking dots to dots to dots to reveal a reindeer or a bow-wrapped box.

We lived on a tiny army post in the middle of the Utah desert, so I remember snow—walking home on the last day of school before Christmas break, all my crafts and ornaments stuffed into my satchel. They'd be unpacked, uncrumpled, and displayed from that day until the new year. Despite the cold, though, I cannot think back on a single Christmas and conjure any adjective other than warm.

Not so for our Ebenezer.

When he and the Ghost of Christmas Past first come across young Scrooge, they see a small boy all alone in a cold, empty schoolroom. The campus is all but deserted, his friends gone home to their families, the teachers resting up wherever teachers go when they've a few weeks of freedom. It's important to note that Scrooge actually witnesses two Christmases at his old school. In the first, he is quite young, and we see his imagination occupied with characters from boyhood literature: Ali Baba and Robinson Crusoe. By the second, he is no longer reading but is found "walking up and down despairingly." So we know that being left alone over the holidays was not a one-holiday fluke. This was his little life.

Loneliness and despair.

Is it any wonder he would grow up to want to bury sticks of holly in the hearts of those who shout out cheerful Christmas greetings?

Last Christmas, our school had an early noon release on the last day before break, and one of my seventh-grade boys was forgotten by his father. Not forever, of course, but for at least thirty minutes it was Luis and me waiting for Mr. D to show up. It was cold. It was windy. It was awkward. When that red pickup truck pulled into our school parking lot, I don't know who was more relieved. But again, that was half an hour with a happy ending.

If it's not enough to feel sad for a boy left all alone, let's extrapolate what else that could mean for young Ebenezer's holiday. The fires would not be lit for one boy. Good food would not be prepared for one boy. Imagine, one by one, your friends climb into carriages and carts, embraced by family, while you watch—cold, hungry, and alone. Like every Christmas before, with no hope for anything better next year.

And then—an open door. Light and love and little footsteps of one sent to save him.

Fan.

"I have come to bring you home, dear brother!" said the child, clapping her tiny hands, and bending down to laugh. "To bring you home, home, home!"

"Home, little Fan?" returned the boy.

"Yes," said the child, brimful of glee. "Home for good and all! Home for ever and ever."

In a snippet of dialogue, we learn that Mr. Scrooge Senior has not always—maybe not ever—been a kind man, but little Fan has softened his heart. He's kinder now, so much so that their home is like heaven, and she's orchestrated a welcome for him there.

This scene is just a tiny preview of Scrooge's true reconciliation: to his earthly father now, to his heavenly Father later this very night. And by bringing Scrooge to witness this moment, the Ghost of Christmas Past works as a conduit to that end. Little Fan may have been the person to bring young Ebenezer back to the Scrooge home, but it is the Ghost of Christmas Past—this embodiment of the duality of God the Father and Christ the Savior—through whom Scrooge makes his first steps to his eternity.

Colossians 1:19–23 tells us that God in all his fullness was pleased to live in Christ, and through him God reconciled everything to himself. He made peace with everything in heaven and on earth by means of Christ's blood on the cross. This includes those of us who were once away from God. We were his enemies, separated from him by evil thoughts and actions.

In other words, this includes any covetous old sinner.

But, Paul warns, you must continue to believe this truth and stand firmly in it. Don't drift away from the assurance you received when you heard the Good News.

That warm, idyllic childhood home I remember? I remember all the goodness of it. At Christmas it was filled with the scent of a real evergreen tree, the sweetness of my mother's cooking, the glow of candles providing soft light all evening. If I had my way, we would have kept the house just like that throughout the year. Everything seems a little more beautiful illuminated by strings of tree lights. The world is softened in a cloud of cinnamon and sugar. There are treats and songs and TV shows that we relegate to the Christmas season, when really we need them all year long.

Fan says Ebenezer is going home forever and that home is like heaven. I would have said mine was too. For seasons at a time. But, of course, their home isn't heaven, no more than mine. And Scrooge doesn't stay there forever. He drifts away. We know Scrooge's father to be an imperfect man who can therefore offer only imperfect, temporary peace. Only Christ, through the sacrifice of his blood, offers a perfect eternal home.

Forever and ever.

Little Fan knows that peace. She will grow up to marry and have a son, Fred, who loves Christmas.

Ebenezer grows up too.

On the arm of the Ghost of Christmas Past we see him—up, up, and away.

7

Old Fezziwig

If I can't throw a good [Christmas] party for my employees,
then I'm a terrible boss. Who wants a drink?

Michael Scott, *The Office*

ears ago, sometime midsummer, my husband, Mikey,
and I posed a question at the dinner table to our three
boys: "What did you get for Christmas last year?" We left
unspoken, you know, all the things that consumed our budget. All
the doodads that sent us into screaming fights about priorities and
luxuries? All the stuff? Alllllllll the stuffffffff. The twins were twelve
years old, the youngest eight. They just sort of stared at us, thinking.

Sega? No, that was your birthday.

Bikes? Nope, Christmas before.

Legos? Well, obviously. That's every year.

"And so," we said in triumph, "this year? No gifts. None. Instead"—
one of us jumped in before the howling could commence—"we're
going to Disneyland. Because memories last forever."

Let me just say that Christmas at Disneyland is not for the faint
of heart. You have to really love you some Christmas to stomach it.
Garland, everywhere. Tinsel, everywhere. All the characters wear tacky
sweaters, and zippy carols stream from all the speakers hidden in the
rocks and pathways of the lands. The most egregious display (if indeed
Christmas decorations can be egregious) is the Small World ride. It's
a Small World is my hands-down favorite Disney experience—all the
little dolls, the dancing, the song. The song. The song. At Christmas,
though, the song is switched to an overlapping medley of "It's a Small
World" and "Jingle Bells." Moreover, all the dolls are stripped of
practically all color and dressed in white. The overall effect set me,
a lover of Christmas, a bit on edge. It seemed intrusive to wash the
entire Small World in the Christmas spirit, knowing full well that in
the Large World some countries don't celebrate Christmas at all.

"Are they all supposed to be dead?" my youngest son asked. "And
are we in, like, Small World heaven?"

Thus, I've given up ideas of going to Disney at Christmastime again.

Bringing to mind this question: If, as Christians, we celebrate
Christmas as a time to acknowledge and worship Christ, is it possible
to celebrate too much? To worship too much? We've managed to build
our nation's economy on a resounding "NO!"

But Jesus? Matthew records a few worship guidelines in chapter 6,
for example: "Be careful not to practice your righteousness in front of
others to be seen by them" (v. 1); "When you give to the needy, do not
announce it with trumpets, as the hypocrites do in the synagogues and
on the streets, to be honored by others" (v. 2).

For purposes of argument, let's take the verbs *celebrate* and
worship out of the equation and gift ourselves with a whole new verb.

Christmas. Back to the question—Can we
Christmas too much?

Once Ebenezer is rescued from
the loneliness of a Christmas away
at school, the Ghost of Christmas
Past takes him to a place every
twenty-something-year-old
longs to be. His job. It is the
prime of Scrooge's life, and he's
gainfully and happily apprenticed
at a warehouse overseen by
old Fezziwig. (A century and a
half later, Jim Hensen's muppet
Fozzie the Bear would play the role
of Fozziwig, which I think is one of
Dickens's best moments of foresight.)

Old Fezziwig puts on the company Christmas
party to end all company Christmas parties. He Christmasses like no
one has ever Christmassed before.

> The warehouse was as snug, and warm, and dry, and bright a ball-room
> as you would desire to see upon a winter's night.
>
> In came a fiddler with a music-book. . . .
>
> There were more dances, and there were forfeits, and more dances,
> and there was cake, and there was negus, and there was a great piece of
> Cold Roast, and there was a great piece of Cold Boiled, and there were
> mince-pies, and plenty of beer.

Granted, this wouldn't be the perfect work Christmas party for
me. I teach at a small private Southern Baptist Christian school, so
dancing would be out even if the faculty women didn't outnumber

the men twenty-three to one. But I do like cake, and a quick google of the word *negus* makes it sound appealing. I've eaten enough midprice catered chicken meals to appreciate a piece of cold boiled, and I'll let you all search your hearts about the beer. Still, by all standards, a rousing way to celebrate the season. To Christmas. One would think the warmth of Fezziwig's hospitality, not to mention the "positive light [that] appeared to issue from Fezziwig's calves" would have an impact on Scrooge. Having come from a childhood in which Christmas was a gray, lonely, cold affair, why would this blazin', fiddlin', eatin', and dancin' shindig not lodge in his heart and inspire him to keep Christmas?

The invisible Scrooge "acted like a man out of his wits. His heart and soul were in the scene, and with his former self. He corroborated everything, remembered everything." The Ghost points out that it was indeed "a small matter . . . to make these silly folks so full of gratitude." And Scrooge agrees. It was a small matter—music, food, laughter. But that small matter didn't allow Christmas to take root in Scrooge because those aren't the matters that root us in Christ. These are the trimmings of Christmas, tinsel draped on the branches of a rootless tree. They are an annoyance to Scrooge because they hold no meaning for him. Fezziwig's party conforms to the pattern of the world. Scrooge needs to be transformed by the renewing of his mind (Rom. 12:2).

Now, I have no reason to doubt Fezziwig's heart. (Or Mrs. Fezziwig's, that lucky woman.)

He appears a kind and generous man, extending hospitality and fellowship in the name of Christ. There's no reason to think that Christ is not treasured in his heart, but his party—all the food, the lights, the music—these are earthly treasures. And, for Scrooge at least, we know that they eventually rusted. Moths of miserliness ate most of them.

And the rest were stolen away.

8

Belle, with a Full Heart

here have been some truly terrible things that have happened to great works of art. Michelangelo's *David* dressed with a fig leaf, the Spanish "restorer" Cecelia Gimenez "fixing" the fresco of Jesus, and the song "When Love Is Gone" cut from the DVD and streaming versions of *The Muppet Christmas Carol*. Those who didn't get a chance to see the movie in theaters or who missed out on the first round of VHS tapes might never get a chance to hear this beautiful, haunting love song performed by the actor playing young Ebenezer and his beautiful Belle.

I say it's a love song because I always think breakup songs speak to the truest of love. Chicago's "If You Leave Me Now," in which a couple faces the fact that neither wants the other to go, and that no matter the argument, the morning light will bring regret for things said in the night—well, it just kills me every time I hear it. The lyric "If you leave me now, you'll take away the very heart of me"[1] acknowledges the kind of love that lets you forgive the person who buys the shiny Scotch tape for Christmas-present wrapping rather than the matte tape that was so very clearly noted in the text message.

But I digress.

Belle and Ebenezer are breaking up. Long before Beyonce would tell the world to "put a ring on it," Belle gave Ebenezer the boot. Why? Because Ebenezer can't commit. No, he's not seeing other women; Belle has been displaced by another idol. "A golden one."

Belle understands what Ebenezer does not: "No one can serve two masters. Either you will hate the one and love the other, or you will be devoted to the one and despise the other." Jesus finishes with a statement of finality: "You cannot serve both God and money" (Matt. 6:24).

Belle is forcing Ebenezer to make this choice.

And the worst part is they aren't just dating. They have an understanding. A contract. In the time that Dickens wrote *A Christmas Carol*, such a contract held a strong intentionality to the promise of marriage. She was, save for the paperwork, his bride. Neither could pursue another relationship without scrutiny and scandal. Belle concedes that their contract is "an old one. It was made when we were both poor and content to be so, until, in good season, we could improve our worldly fortune by our patient industry. You *are* changed. When it was made, you were another man."

"I was a boy," Ebenezer says.

Remember Ebenezer as a boy? Freshly restored to his father's home? Dancing at Fezziwig's party? That means, too, that Belle was a girl. She has ostensibly spent her entire life waiting for Ebenezer

1. Peter Cetera, "If You Leave Me Now," *Chicago X*, Columbia Records, June 14, 1976.

to marry her. She has shut herself away from any other opportunity for love. For her to walk away from this commitment, to risk her reputation and face the terrifying prospect of a middle-class Victorian woman without a husband, shows the deepest understanding of all. She tells Ebenezer, "You fear the world too much." She fears it not at all.

Ebenezer makes no effort to stop her from leaving. He makes lame attempts to defend his choices, but in the end allows Belle to release him with "a full heart, for the love of him you once were," wishing him to be "happy in the life you have chosen."

"She left him; and they parted."

Ebenezer walks away from his bride.

When Jesus encounters a rich young Ebenezer ruler, as recorded in Matthew 19:16–22, he is confronted with the question of what the young man must do to have eternal life. Jesus answers, telling the young man to obey all the commandments, which the young ruler has done, and then Jesus brings it home with this zinger: "If you want to be perfect, go, sell your possessions and give to the poor, and you will have treasure in heaven. Then come, follow me."

When the rich young man heard this, "he went away sad, because he had great wealth."

The ruler walked away from a commitment to Christ. And I think it's safe to say that Jesus walked away too.

They parted from each other.

This is the moment when most film adaptations of *A Christmas Carol* bring the heartbroken Scrooge back to his bed, the visit with the Ghost of Christmas Past having accomplished its purpose. But the novel has one final scene in Scrooge's journey through the past—this one the most painful of all.

Seven years earlier. The night of Jacob Marley's death, and Scrooge is standing in the parlor of a bustling household. Belle's household. It is "a room, not very large or handsome, but full of comfort." She has married and is surrounded by joyous, healthy children. It is the only scene in the journey with this Ghost in which the vision of the young Ebenezer Scrooge himself is not present. How can he be? This is the very life he chose to abandon.

Scrooge looks upon Belle, seeing her perhaps for the first time since they parted. Our intrusive narrator guide reassures us of her desirability. He would like "to have touched her lips . . . to have looked upon the lashes of her downcast eyes . . . to have let loose waves of [her] hair." In this moment Scrooge is very much a man of heart and soul and passion, and it is this glimpse of his permanent, eternal separation from Belle—this peek into what he might have had—that breaks him.

There is a reason our hearts break at Christmas. We've spent the rest of the year toughening them up, keeping busy. We can spend months upon months caring nothing for our fellow man because there are no sappy commercials and heartfelt movies to remind us to love them. All of us are susceptible to the same heartbreaking regret Scrooge experiences in this moment. Maybe not a lost love but a broken friendship, a marginalized family member—bitterness left to flourish Christmas after Christmas. Scrooge is separated from Belle by years of silence. Years of living with a bad decision made while his heart was still malleable. This isn't about begrudging the life Belle has been given but about regretting his own foolish choice.

He begs, "Spirit, . . . remove me from this place." To which the Ghost replies with his familiar refrain, "These [are] the shadows of the things that have been. . . .That they are what they are, do not blame me."

Scrooge cannot bear it. There is a struggle—if one can truly struggle with a Spirit—and Scrooge grasps the Spirit's cap, pressing it down and down and down. "The Spirit dropped beneath it, so that the extinguisher covered its whole form; but though Scrooge pressed it down with all his force, he could not hide the light, which streamed from under it, in an unbroken flood upon the ground."

The Light is unbroken.

9

The Empty Scabbard
Christ in His Brother

For unto us a child is born, unto us a son is given: and the government
shall be upon his shoulder: and his name shall be called Wonderful,
Counsellor, The mighty God, The everlasting Father, The Prince of Peace.

Isaiah 9:6 KJV

f you aren't humming bars of Handel's *Messiah* right
now, I have to doubt the depth of your Christmas
spirit.

King of Kings!
Hallelujah! Hallelujah!
And Lord of Lords!
Hallelujah! Hallelujah!

The prophet Isaiah previews the Messiah twofold: as the child who would be born and as the King who would reign forever.

And ever! And ever!
Hallelujah! Hallelujah!

At the time of the prophet's writing, the Son lives but is not yet given; his immortality extends before and beyond this time. In between these stretches of eternity, the Son is born, lives, and dies— his flesh and humanity as tangible as that of any man. He can be seen, touched, heard.

And Scrooge hears him.

While the first Spirit of Christmas imposed itself on Scrooge, hovering at his bedside, flooding him with light, the Spirit of Christmas Present beckons. Roused from sleep at the strike of the clock, Scrooge lies in the darkness, restless within "a blaze of ruddy light . . . which being only light, was more alarming than a dozen ghosts." Scrooge leaves his bed to investigate, tiptoes through the house. "The moment Scrooge's hand was on the lock, a strange voice called him by his name, and bade him to enter. He obeyed."

He comes into his own room, yet not his room. He has walked into Christmas. The walls look like a perfect grove, covered in living green—holly, mistletoe, and ivy, with glistening berries akin to little mirrors reflecting back the light. There is a blazing fire roaring up the chimney, the likes that had never been seen in all of Scrooge's days there—or Marley's, for that matter. The floor is heaped with a feast: every kind of meat, fruit, pies, punch. In short, it's like watching an hour of Hallmark on TV, without the soft focus on the aging actress. It's every commercial for the Honey Baked Ham Company and Glade candles and Pillsbury cookies and Target.

Inescapable overabundance. After all, Jesus said, "I have come that they may have life, and have it to the full" (John 10:10).

Right now, "they" is Scrooge.

In his initial description, the Ghost of Christmas Present seems more like a forerunner of a commercialized Father Christmas than a metaphorical composite of Jesus Christ. Scrooge finds "a jolly Giant, glorious to see, who bore a glowing torch, in shape not unlike Plenty's horn, and held it up, high up, to shed its light on Scrooge, as he came peeping round the door."

"'Come in!' exclaimed the Ghost. 'Come in, and know me better, man!'"

I cannot read this scene without flashing back to the rousing revival services of my childhood. The congregation singing verse after verse of "Just As I Am" and "I Surrender All." After an hour's preaching, those convicted of their sin, made aware of a need of a Savior, poured down the aisle, tears running down their cheeks.

The Ghost is affable, generous, welcoming. His eyes are clear and kind, and yet Scrooge, still the covetous old sinner, was loath to meet them.

But the Spirit insists. "Look upon me!"

And Scrooge does so, reverently.

Dickens is no less detailed in the symbolism of Christ in this Spirit than he was in his description of the first, although now we see a man, unmistakably human, in the prime of his life. He is clothed in a green robe—again, the color of eternal life—lined with the white fur of sinlessness. The garment hangs loose and open, revealing that his "capacious breast was bare, as if disdaining to be warded or concealed by any artifice." Side note: it's always bothersome to me when this Spirit is portrayed as a man who's been indulging in too many eggnogs and pumpkin pies. He is not, for lack of a better word, fat. Years of synonymizing "jolly" with "jiggle" has led people to believe this Spirit should be ho-ho-hoing in the midst of his magical buffet. This glimpse into the Spirit's physique emphasizes his humanity. He is skin and bone and muscle. His feet, too, are bare—a nod to the fact that, as human as he is, there exists a transcendent quality to his flesh. It's Christmas Eve in London, and he is impervious to the cold. Moreover, the bare breast and feet hearken to that familiar image of Jesus on the cross, his body exposed, his feet pierced. And the imagery doesn't end there. Where Christ on the cross wears a crown of thorns, this Christmas Spirit wears "a holly wreath, set here and there with shining icicles."

King of Kings.

"Girded round its middle was an antique scabbard; but no sword was in it, and the ancient sheath was eaten up with rust."

Prince of Peace.

He is not, however, forever and ever. Not in this incarnation. He is one of more than eighteen hundred brothers (1843 to be exact—get it? Get it? Because we number our calendar years according to his life on earth?) He is finite. At this one o'clock hour, he is very young; by the end of his time with Scrooge, he will be very old; and during the time in-between, we will see him being everything to Scrooge that Jesus is to the world.

Scrooge is submissive, ready to be conducted wherever the Spirit takes him. It is a journey of spiritual healing, and it begins where so many others experienced the healing of Jesus.

With a touch of his robe.

10

A Peculiar Flavor Sprinkled from the Torch

crooge in his nightdress and cap and the Ghost of Christmas Present with his generous green robe and locks of flowing brown hair walk through the streets of London that Christmas morning. Shops are closing, though their windows still display enticing wares. People hustle and bustle about, and at the rare instance of a quarrel, the Ghost sprinkles incense from his torch on the conversation, restoring their good humor. "For they said, it was a shame to quarrel upon Christmas Day. And so it was! God love it, so it was!"

Scrooge asks if there is a particular flavor in what the Ghost sprinkles from his torch.

"There is," he says. "My own."

That, my friends, is the spirit of Christmas.

Indefinable, right? That something in the air. The first Christmas commercial on TV. "Chestnuts roasting on an open fire . . ." when you're running into the store for milk and toilet paper. We have a favorite Chinese food restaurant, and come December there's a mini Christmas tree and Nativity scene wedged between the statues of Buddha. Somehow we all get used to having giant evergreens in the middle of our living rooms. The whole world sounds like sleigh bells and smells like cookies.

Joyful. Delicious.

Scrooge is being led in a triumphal procession, while the Spirit spreads the fragrance of Christmas everywhere. Literally, everywhere. As Scrooge touches his robe, he is led to the humble hut of a miner, one who toils in the bowels of the earth, sharing a simple Christmas dinner with his children and grandchildren. Then above the moors to the sea, where two lighthouse keepers join hands and wish each other a Merry Christmas. Then out to the sea itself, to a ship atop the churning waters, where sailors hum Christmas tunes and speak of Christmases gone by. Wherever the Spirit goes, he is welcome. He is perfectly suited, perfectly sized.

He is the flavor of Christ, and Scrooge is caught up in the scent. I know this Scripture isn't exactly part of Dickens's original manuscript, but I can just picture these two guys, strolling through the streets, zipping through the air, the Ghost of Christmas Present speaking out:

> Thanks be to God, who in Christ always leads us in triumphal procession, and through us spreads the fragrance of the knowledge of him everywhere. For we are the aroma of Christ to God among those who are being saved and among those who are perishing, to one a fragrance from death to death, to the other a fragrance from life to life. Who is sufficient for these things? For we are not, like so many, peddlers of God's word, but as men of sincerity, as commissioned by God, in the sight of God we speak in Christ. (2 Cor. 2:14–17 ESV)

Scrooge and Spirit: men of sincerity.

So what does it take to be the aroma of Christ?

Years ago, my mother worked as our church secretary, and part of her job meant giving money to the indigent of our town from the office cash set aside for that purpose. Over time, she got to know a particular young man who lived—and worked, selling himself—on the streets in a particularly unsavory neighborhood. Over time, she saw him deteriorate, growing pale and sickly thin. One winter night he came, his weak body overcome with a wracking, wet cough, his face riddled with sores. Of course, he hadn't been to a doctor or to a clinic. He'd come to my mother to see if he could get something for his fever and money to pay for a bed on a cold night. Then, for some mysterious reason, he asked her, "Will you touch me? Will you feel my heart?"

Mom did. She felt the heat of his fever burning through his shirt. She felt his breath working its way through his lungs. She felt his heart. This was the mid-1980s, and she knew. She'd seen the news reports of the mysterious epidemic killing young men, and here he seemed to be the disease's latest victim. This was the time when the AIDS virus was an unknown, frightful thing. A time when society, as the Spirit of Christmas Present said, was defined by "deeds of passion, pride, ill-will, hatred, envy, bigotry, and selfishness in our name." A time when not many people would have touched this young man. But my mother did. If she'd taken the time to think, to consider, to respond in her own flesh, she might have kept her touch to herself. Instead, she allowed the Holy Spirit to guide her hand. She touched him in the very manner the first Ghost touched Scrooge, and the young man was upheld. Mom was the aroma of Christ to one who was perishing, and she never saw him again.

On that dark December night, the aroma of Christmas filled the room. Imagine the fragrance of the world if we all reached out to those who so desperately need to feel the love of Christ.

None of this seems nearly as Christmas-y as the rollickingly humble dinner at the Cratchits' house (we'll get to that) or the festival of snarky parlor games at nephew Fred's (we'll get there too), but too often we're ready to dive into the tinsel and frosting and the rocking around the Christmas tree and forget that Silent Nights can be silent because they are sad. But Holy Nights are holy because they are sweet.

11

Bob Cratchit's Dwelling

or some, preparations for Christmas dinner begin roughly the moment the Thanksgiving dishes are drying by the sink. Our social media feeds fill with recipes and picture-perfect photographs of tantalizing turkeys and steaming bowls of stuffing. Both of my sisters are blessed with the love and talent for making treats, and they spend December rolling out cookies and boiling concoctions to hard-crack stages and foil-wrapping cakes to freeze until Christmas Eve, when the fruits of their labor will be plated and lined up along three dining room tables. Their favorite tradition? The night-before toast tearing for the stuffing. (Or, dressing, if you prefer.)

Somehow, that particular gene skipped me. When I procrastinate too long to get a good reservation downtown, I'm scrambling at the last minute, fighting through the aisles with a shopping cart full of good intentions and Stove Top stuffing. I must say, I enjoyed the process of the holiday meal a lot more when the pressures of social media didn't foster this sort of competition—friends tweeting about how amazing the house smells, posting their perfect pie, and Instagram full of centerpieces and good dishes.

I have a little holiday dinner tradition I've adopted in the last few years. Thanksgiving and Christmas Day, sometime around noon, I put this post out on Facebook: What did you forget to buy at the grocery store that you're just going to do without? The answers vary.

Sugar-free Cool Whip

Vegan butter

Fresh rosemary

Sour cream

Extra bacon for the asparagus (not the same people wanting vegan butter)

Psalm 22:26 says, "The meek shall eat and be satisfied" (ESV). And there isn't a family richer in meekness than the Cratchits. Mrs. Cratchit has toiled all day on the day's supper: goose, stuffing, mashed potatoes, gravy, applesauce, pudding. A poor man's feast. A simple meal for a shabby family. There's Mr. Cratchit (Bob), underappreciated and underpaid; Mrs. Cratchit (Mrs. Cratchit) in her years-old dress that she's tried to update with cheap ribbons; Martha, the eldest, who is late to her family dinner because she has had to work late preparing the Christmas feast of her employer; Peter, wearing his father's oversized shirt, stealing a bit of potato and wishing he could show off his finery in a fashionable park; Belinda, the next oldest daughter, learning the same skills as her mother because she will probably live the same life as her mother; and two other little ones—a boy and a girl—unnamed because, let's face it, in these Victorian days, at least one of them isn't long for this world.

Oh, and, of course, Tiny Tim. With his little crutch and his sweet singing voice and his heartfelt "God bless us every one" as the family drinks hot stuff from the jug while chestnuts sputter and crack noisily on the fire.

Scrooge has remained silent for the entirety of the meal, offering
no comment on the size of the goose, or the thinness of the gravy,
or the responsibility of the applesauce to eke out enough for all. He
is unfazed by the small pudding, blazing in half of half-a-quartern
of ignited brandy with Christmas holly stuck into the top. The old
Scrooge, the Scrooge of Christmas Eve, might have wanted to see Tiny
Tim boiled alongside the pudding when he softly wishes a Christmas
blessing. But this Scrooge implores the Spirit "with an interest he had
never felt before, 'Tell me if Tiny Tim will live.'"

He does not ask if Martha and Belinda will find and marry men as
kind and loving as their father. He does not wonder if Peter will learn a
trade. He doesn't look at the little, nameless ones, who are undoubtedly
sickly and thin, and beg for assurance that they, too, will thrive. Nor
does the Spirit offer any assurance. The family, after all, are the meek
who, according to Jesus Christ, will inherit the earth (Matt. 5:5). They
will be blessed for their humility, their cheerful contentment. They are
the fruits of the Spirit and the Beatitudes all rolled up into one.

Okay, so Mrs. Cratchit is a little bitter around the edges, but she's
the one pinning bows on her sleeve in an effort to hold her dress
together because her husband's boss won't pay salary enough to afford
both food and clothing. Still, when pressed, she offers a begrudging
blessing to Mr. Scrooge, the "Founder of the Feast."

Scrooge, however, remains laser-focused on Tiny Tim. Why?
Because the family, in all their fruit-filled beatitudiness, are invisible
to him. They have an essence he can't even fathom. Tiny Tim is all of
this, too, but his future is measurably dire. As the Spirit says, "If these
shadows remain unaltered by the Future, the child will die."

Scrooge protests, "Oh no, kind Spirit! Say he will be spared!"

To which the Spirit throws Scrooge's own words back into his face:
"What then? If he be like to die, he had better do it, and decrease the
surplus population."

In response, Scrooge hangs his head.

My mother has a saying: "You rarely regret words you do not say." We toss around the idea that our words can come back to haunt us, and here is Scrooge, in the shadow of a Spirit, haunted by his words. Sometimes the turn of phrase that seems so harmless and clever in a vacuum becomes a monster when it crosses paths with a life. Grand proclamations diminish under the lens of humanity. You know that feeling—that awful, face-chilling feeling—when you've been caught in a lie? Know what's worse? Being trapped by something you used to think was the truth. And here, pinned by his own words, Scrooge is squirming.

Still, these words serve a purpose. They create an indelible bond between Scrooge and the child; the desire for Tiny Tim to live overpowers Scrooge's previous belief that he should die. As pure-spirited as Tiny Tim may be on the inside, on the outside he is crippled, wounded, dying. With the first of the Spirits, Scrooge saw himself as a child. Now, when he sees this child, he sees himself.

And now there are two lives to be reclaimed.

12

Here Is a New Game

It is a fair, even-handed, noble adjustment of things, that while there is infection in disease and sorrow, there is nothing in the world so irresistibly contagious as laughter and good-humour.

A Christmas Carol

few years ago, our church put on a musical production of *A Christmas Carol* that included a number featuring the Ghost of Christmas Present and Scrooge. The Ghost was actually called the Angel of Christmas Present so as not to offend anybody other than those well acquainted with the novel, but this was just one of the liberties taken with Dickens's original text. The Ghost/Angel was appropriately costumed with a long beard and green robe. He delivered his lines with a fitting jocularity and unnecessary Irish accent. The song they performed was nothing less than a drinking song. The two toasted each other with mugs of grog while performing an Irish-ish jig. They drank and danced and danced and drank until

Scrooge was a collapsed pile of inebriation. Cute, right? Part of me bristles at the fact that the playwright won't use the word *Ghost* but has no problem turning the embodiment of Christ into a high-fivin', hard-drinkin' cultural cliché, but I digress.

The Christmas party at Fred's is, in every way, the opposite of the Christmas gathering at the Cratchits' while simultaneously creating a perfect parallel. Where Mrs. Cratchit ekes out a modest dinner for eight, Fred and his wife (affectionately known as "Scrooge's Niece"— what has Dickens got against naming his minor female characters?) host a party of twenty. Scrooge and the Spirit arrive, fresh from their dark and deadly ocean tour, to find Fred midjoke at Scrooge's expense.

"Ha, ha! Ha, ha, ha, ha!"

"He said that Christmas was a humbug, as I live! . . . He believed it too!"

(Pause for laughter.)

Fred's wife, exceedingly pretty as she may be, finds no humor in her husband's tale. She may be young and fashionable, but in spirit she is a mirror image of Mrs. Cratchit. She'll have none of this lighthearted portrayal of this man who should feel shame. Cratchit's wife complains that Scrooge doesn't pay her husband enough; Fred's wife complains that Scrooge isn't bequeathing his nephew enough. Just as Bob Cratchit softly cajoles his wife into wishing Scrooge a begrudging Merry Christmas, Fred presses his own case for pity.

"He's a comical old fellow, that's the truth: and not so pleasant as he might be. However, his offences carry their own punishment, and I have nothing to say against him."

Currently the punishment for his offenses is made entirely of missing out on this party. They have food, drinks, dessert, music, singing, games. True, the games are thinly veiled excuses for the lascivious Topper to foist unwanted advances on Scrooge's niece's sister ("the plump one"—really, Charles?). They play a handsy game of blind man's bluff, filling the room with laughter.

Fred's voice rises above the flirty fray: "I mean to give him the same chance every year, whether he likes it or not, for I pity him. He may rail at Christmas till he dies, but he can't help thinking better of it—I defy him."

As discouraging as it might be to have his awful uncle refuse his Christmas invitation year after year, Fred persists. Why? It's not because Uncle Ebenezer would bring new life to the party. Who wants to watch an old man wear a blindfold and chase a girl around a sofa? He'd bring nothing in the way of entertainment, unless he somehow learns to set his money counting to music. Fred persists because it is the right thing to do: not for Scrooge, not for Fred, not for his plump sister-in-law. It's the right thing to do for Bob Cratchit. After all, Fred says, "If it only puts him in the vein to leave his poor clerk fifty pounds, *that's* something."

The apostle Paul urges in Galatians 6:9: "Let us not grow weary of doing good, for in due season we will reap, if we do not give up" (ESV).

Fred will not give up.

Sure, he would like to have a relationship with his uncle. Such might be beneficial now, and even more so when Scrooge names an heir to his modest fortune. But Fred expresses no interest in his own financial gain, seeming nothing but content with a life rich with friendship. His house is full of love and laughter this Christmas— twenty guests that he knows of, and one more observing from the shadows.

While visiting the past at Fezziwig's party, Scrooge's slipper-clad feet tapped silently with the dancers. Here, he cheers on his niece by marriage and shouts out answers to the wordplay games. Like a child, he begs to stay out later—"One half hour, Spirit, only one!"

With this, the Ghost is pleased. "If [there is] any encouragement from being united with Christ, if any comfort from his love, if any common sharing in the Spirit, if any tenderness and compassion, then make my joy complete by being like-minded, having the same love, being one in spirit and of one mind" (Phil. 2:1–2).

If Scrooge could have had his way, he would have remained an invisible thread in the fabric of Fred's wife's curtains until the last guest bid good night. But, of course, they cannot stay. Fred unknowingly sends him off in a toast: "A Merry Christmas and a Happy New Year to the old man, whatever he is! He wouldn't take it from me, but may he have it nevertheless. Uncle Scrooge!"

And they are gone. They visit sickbeds, almshouses, foreign lands, prisons—every place where man had not barred the Spirit out. A long night, indeed so much more than a night. Scrooge and the Spirit have visited many homes, leaving all with a happy end. Thousands of lives; hundreds of faces. Exhausting by any measure, but not over yet. There are two more left to meet.

13

Within the Robe

Ignorance

e have a painting in the big, sweeping connective hallway of our church. It's massive (four feet by ten feet), depicting Jesus, sitting, surrounded by children. Jesus looks the way you would expect Jesus to look under these circumstances. His hair is neat and long(ish), his beard trim, his eyes soft and brown. His face is round and joyous; he looks like he's just heard something utterly delightful.

The children, too, look like the children you would see in a painting in the hallway adjacent to a state-of-the-art nursery. A healthy mix of boys and girls—healthy being the operative word. They have chubby cheeks and fat l'il legs. Ten fingers, ten toes, bright eyes. They are dressed in play clothes. Some toddle, some clamber, some contentedly play with flowers at Jesus's sturdy, sandal-clad feet.

The picture is one of idyllic, inclusive access. It is a sincere attempt to be the embodiment of Matthew 19:14, when Jesus admonishes the disciples and says, "Let the little children come to me, and do not hinder them, for the kingdom of heaven belongs to such as these."

The Jesus and children of this painting have zero resemblance to the children we see clinging to the Ghost of Christmas Present as his hours on earth come to an end.

It has been quite a round of Christmas celebrations. The Cratchits' dinner, Fred's party, the ocean . . . and to top it off, a children's Twelfth Night party. Kind of like a calendar for the entire month of December condensed into one night. Or one day? Or one day and night? Or . . . time is tricky in this story. And while Scrooge remains unchanged (in his outward form—wink, wink), the Spirit has clearly grown older. His hair has turned gray—must've been the children's party that sent him over the edge.

The life span of the Spirit solidifies the idea that he is one of more than eighteen hundred brothers. If we measure the year from Christmas to Christmas, every year is new. The old one passes on. Too, it hearkens back to the mortality of Jesus Christ. He did not grow old, but his life came to an end, and we measure our years from that appointed time.

The Spirit's life ends tonight, at midnight, and somewhere a clock is chiming away his last fifteen minutes.

That's when Scrooge notices something peeking out from the Spirit's robe and is prompted to ask, "Is it a foot or a claw?" And then, from his robe, the Spirit brings two children: "wretched, abject, frightful, hideous, miserable. They knelt down at its feet, and clung upon the outside of its garment."

These children are so hideous, so disturbing—Scrooge cannot bear to look at them. But the Spirit compels him.

"They were a boy and a girl. Yellow, meagre, ragged, scowling, wolfish. . . . Where graceful youth should have filled their features out, and touched them with its freshest tints, a stale and shrivelled hand, like that of age, had pinched, and twisted them, and pulled them into shreds. Where angels might have sat enthroned, devils lurked, and glared out menacing."

Guarantee: you will never see that scene depicted in pastels on the walls of your church nursery.

These children have names: the boy is Ignorance; the girl is Want. And they belong to us.

"Beware them both," says the Spirit, "and all of their degree, but most of all beware this boy, for on his brow I see that written which is Doom, unless the writing be erased."

Note that the Spirit doesn't say "beware *of* the boy." Scrooge has nothing to fear from this wretched, ignorant creature. In essence, the Spirit is telling Scrooge to be aware—to look upon him, to face him, to acknowledge him—because if Scrooge does not, the boy is doomed. Now, doomed to what, exactly?

Consider the context of the story for a moment. Scrooge has not outwardly changed, but inwardly, his transformation—his reclamation—is already well in hand. He has been given a chance that the boy has not. But there is still time for the boy. The damning message of ignorance can be erased.

There is hope, and that hope is Scrooge, because Scrooge has taken a first step out of his own ignorance. At this moment he is no longer the squeezing, wrenching, grasping, scraping, clutching, covetous old sinner! But he did not become such in a vacuum: he is very much the product of his time, and he represents the totality of his city—London. A place of immense power. And wealth. And ignorance. And want. Dickens's message to Scrooge here is a message to the city herself. To the audience of this story. If Scrooge, and the people like him—the people who have paid a pretty pound for this beautifully bound book— deny the fact that they (and you, and we) bear the responsibility for changing the fate of this child; if they (you, we) slander the truth of this message, then they (you, we) make the fate of that child worse.

Scrooge has been called out. Singled out. Chosen from all the other heartless, greedy men of business and given an opportunity to be free from his chains. All those phantoms floating outside his window were just as ignorant as this boy. They are the ugliness that the boy grows into. They are eternally fettered to doom. "They are darkened in their understanding and separated from the life of God because of the ignorance that is in them due to the hardening of their hearts" (Eph. 4:18).

Scrooge could have remained in such darkness, but that is not the way he has learned from the Spirit of Christmas. He has heard, he's been taught. He is poised to put off his old self, which belongs to his former life (v. 22). He's ready to step away from his corruption. He's primed for a renewal of his mind. He's measured up for a new persona—something like the likeness of God: righteous and holy.

And the very next words out of his mouth prove it.

14

Within the Robe

Want

[Interior: Scrooge's Office. Evening]

Collector of Charity: Many thousands are in want of common
　　　　necessaries; hundreds of thousands are in want of common
　　　　comforts, sir.

Scrooge: [sneeringly] Are there no prisons?

Collector of Charity: Plenty of prisons.

Scrooge: And the Union workhouses? Are they still in operation?

Collector of Charity: [resigned] They are. Still, I wish I could say they
　　　　were not.

Scrooge: [sarcastically] Oh! I was afraid that something had occurred to
　　　　stop them in their useful course.

[Cut to Exterior: Night. An abandoned London street, snow-covered,
　　　　dark. Ebenezer Scrooge stands beside the towering figure of the
　　　　Ghost of Christmas Present, now aged, with a gray beard and
　　　　long, iron-gray hair. At the feet of the Ghost are two ragged,

emaciated children, clinging to his robe. They are Ignorance and Want.]

Scrooge: [trembling] Spirit, are they yours?

Ghost: [voice weak] They are Man's. And they cling to me, appealing from their fathers.

Scrooge: Have they no refuge or resource?

Ghost: [summoning the very last of his strength] Are there no prisons? Are there no workhouses?

[Bell Strikes Twelve]

When I teach *A Christmas Carol*, my students go nuts at this moment in the movie. They hoot, "Ooooh!! Burrrnnn!" because what is more satisfying than seeing a villain's own words used against him? It's the ultimate insult. It's the pinnacle of "I know you are, but what am I?" It's almost like the kids are waiting for the Spirit to bust out with something insulting about Scrooge's mother.

I let them enjoy the moment. After all, we're usually watching the film on the last day before Christmas break. They are sugared up on candy canes, and I have a gift bag full of teacher Christmas gifts—Starbucks cards, candles, cool pens, and comfy socks. We're all just ready to go. But there's far more to this moment than the Spirit's clapback.

Yes, hearing the ugliness of Scrooge's heartless greed spoken by the symbolic embodiment of Christ is jarring. This, we want to say, is the moment of Scrooge's conviction. The moment he recognizes and repents of his sinful nature. After all, these are the Spirit's final words coming from the same guy who hours before sat on top of an entire buffet's worth of food and beckoned Scrooge to his side. It's like the Spirit has been just waiting for this moment to drop the best bon mot of his short life. Perfect timing. Impeccable delivery.

Bell strikes twelve.

Mic drop.

Spirit out.

Except, it isn't. Meaning, this isn't the moment that turns Scrooge's heart. That happened just a breath before, one line of dialogue above—Scrooge's heart is already broken.

"Have they no refuge or resource?"

These are not the words of Christmas Eve Scrooge. This is a question posed by a man who recognizes Want and wishes to heal it. True, he's not quite at the place to offer up himself and make sacrifices in his life, but he has completely transformed from the man who would want these pitiable waifs to just hurry up and die already. His is the heart of King David, writing in Psalm 51:3–4:

> For I know my transgressions,
>   and my sin is always before me.
> Against you, you only, have I sinned
>   and done what is evil in your sight;
> so you are right in your verdict
>   and justified when you judge.

Through all the wanderings in the past and all the invisible spying on this Christmas, Scrooge has come to his own conclusion.

The Spirits Past and Present have only required Scrooge to look upon himself and those whose lives he touches. There's been no browbeating, no accusations. Not even from Marley, who knows Scrooge better than anyone else on earth-ish. Jesus tells us how fruitless it is to point out our sins to each other. Our eyes have to be open to our own. In this last moment, the Spirit gives Scrooge something to see.

When the Spirit parrots Scrooge's hate-filled words, the intent is not condemnation. The Savior does not pour judgment into a heart broken for him. Instead, the exchange gives Scrooge—and us, the readers—a chance to see the reclaimed Scrooge in full contrast with the lost Scrooge. The first called for prison and workhouses; this new man wishes for resources and refuge. Further, this exemplifies what David writes in verse 4 of the psalm: "Against you, you only, have I sinned." Scrooge's words—spoken from his hardened heart—carried his sin. The Spirit isn't throwing them at Scrooge; they're simply bouncing back.

The Spirit may disappear within the chiming of the clock, but Scrooge will see him again in his eternal form. Then, he will be the King, and he will say to Ebenezer, "Truly I tell you, whatever you did for one of the least of these brothers and sisters of mine, you did for me" (Matt. 25:40).

But that conversation—it's going to be a while coming. The bell might be tolling, but it's not tolling for Scrooge.

At least not yet.

15

ℳ Single ℋand
Christ Emerges from the Darkness

irst, to clarify a common misconception. The Ghost of Christmas Future is not Death. I understand the confusion, because there are some aesthetic overlaps. Towering height. Facelessness. Bony form beneath a long, black hooded gown. The silence. The eeriness. This Spirit alone is identified as a Phantom.

This Spirit does not fall so easily into Christ symbolism. It is not the Eternal Infant of Christmas Past; it is not the Peaceful Warrior of Christmas Present. It offers no words of comfort or encouragement:

> "Bear but a touch of my hand there, and you shall be upheld in more than this."

> "Come in! Come in and know me better, man!"

It offers no words of gentle rebuke:

"I told you these were the shadows of the things that have been. That they are what they are, do not blame me!"

"If these shadows remain unaltered by the Future, the child will die."

It offers only this. Where the Past appeared and the Present beckoned, the Future approaches: "Slowly, gravely, silently." (Gravely—see what Charles did there?)

Scrooge bends down to his knee. No witty banter. (This guy is definitely more grave than gravy.) No arguments. No touching the robe.

"Although well used to ghostly company by this time, Scrooge feared the silent shape so much that his legs trembled beneath him, and he found that he could hardly stand when he prepared to follow it."

This is Scrooge's burning bush. His pillar of fire, his pillar of clouds. This is why God appears to great men in the Bible in their dreams, because he is too holy to look upon otherwise. While the previous Spirits were stitched together from bits of flesh and symbols, this one is stripped to its essence, curtained off like the Holy of Holies, and given just one tiny hint of humanity.

The hand.

In all of the movies, the hand is enormous, tipped with long nails, fingers curved to replicate a gothic version of Michelangelo's *Creation of Adam*. The Phantom scene is underscored by ominous music— lots of bassoon and cello. Scrooge grovels, whiskered chin quivering behind the gliding figure. Often, the films are so bent on creating this macabre moment, they completely miss out on this tiny detail of grace when the Spirit pauses a moment, "as observing his condition, and giving him time to recover."

Not that this makes Scrooge feel any better. He is thrilled with a vague uncertain horror to know that, somewhere in that vast darkness, the eyes of the Spirit are upon him. Which is precisely why, for the purposes of Scrooge's reclamation, the Spirits had to appear in this order. Not just because Past, Present, Future fits our idea of nice, normal chronology but also because the Ebenezer of Christmas Eve would never have survived the scrutiny of this Spirit. This is the Scrooge with the broken heart, and that brokenness brings him to a paradox of cowardly confidence.

"I fear you more than any Spectre I have seen. But as I know your purpose is to do me good, and as I hope to live to be another man from what I was, I am prepared to bear your company, and do it with a thankful heart."

Note: he is prepared to be another man from what he was. Not just a better man but another man altogether.

"So from now on we regard no one from a worldly point of view. Though we once regarded Christ in this way, we do so no longer. Therefore, if anyone is in Christ, the new creation has come: The old has gone, the new is here!" (2 Cor. 5:16–17).

Scrooge's view of the world has been permanently altered. His temporal fear of falling from his window has been replaced with a fear so reverent he can barely stand on solid ground. And while it's easy to interpret his reaction as one of a man afraid to die, he doesn't fear death for death's sake. He fears not being able to live in his new self.

Once again Scrooge implores the Spirit to speak. Once again, the Spirit refuses. Scrooge longs for the comforting companionship of a Christmas voice, because his brokenness is still so new.

I think about the first Christmas my family faced after the death of my older brother. The unevenness of the holiday. We used to be four kids, now we were three. All grown up and married and everything, but still . . . My mother always likes to shop for the common "big" gift.

The year everybody got new Bibles.

The year we all got Birkenstocks.

The year we all got leather coats.

That first Christmas without Chris, she had to shop for the four girls (me, my sisters, and sister-in-law), and the three guys—her sons-in-law. Just . . . off. Of course, we aren't the first family to face Christmas with a loss, and it won't be the last Christmas where we'll find an empty place at the table. One less gift to give, one less gift to receive, one voice absent from the conversation. But fresh brokenness is always the hardest, because all the shards are still sharp. It takes years for them to soften. We've worn ours down with stories and memories, smoothed them with equal parts laughter and tears.

Scrooge says, "Lead on! The night is waning fast, and it is precious time to me, I know." He has learned the life span of the Spirit, that it will end. And we all know the same holds true for us—so moments are precious. Not so much the moments of the past—not all of them, anyway. But all of those that are stretched before us? All those moments of life that are waiting? Precious. Even the ones that are hard. Even those moments that, because of life, because of loss, might seem like moments impossible to get through.

But see what the Spirit does for Scrooge.

"The Phantom moved away as it had come towards him. Scrooge followed in the shadow of its dress, which bore him up, he thought, and carried him along."

When I think of some of my sad Christmases—the first without my brother, the first with a broken family, the years when we had no money, the time when my son was in such a dark, dark place, the first without the grandmother, who has been a part of every Christmas of my life—I have to think of myself as being carried along on the robe of my Christmas Future.

Lead on.

16

One Little Knot
of Businessmen

The poor are shunned even by their neighbors, but the rich have many friends.

Proverbs 14:20

crooge is rich, and Scrooge has friends. Maybe not many, but his solitary-as-an-oyster existence does make a way for a few acquaintances, at least. Fellow men of business: "a great fat man with a monstrous chin"; "a [man] taking a vast quantity of snuff out of a very large snuff-box"; "a red-faced gentleman with a pendulous excrescence on the end of his nose, that shook like the gills of a turkey."

I mean, who needs names when you have such precise, flattering descriptions?

He and the Phantom have sidled up to a conversation and scored
a bit of gossip. A member of the snuff-box-coin-purse-money club
is dead. They wonder about the money. ("Left it to his company,
perhaps. He hasn't left it to *me*.") They comment on the cheapness
of the funeral, whether or not there will be lunch. One who admits
that he never wears black gloves and never eats lunch says he'll go if
somebody will go with him. I, however, doubt his word. Not that he
wouldn't go to the funeral, but that he never eats lunch, because this
line is spoken by the large man with the monstrous chin, and you don't
get a monstrous chin by skipping lunch. Just sayin'. Still, he reflects
that he may be Scrooge's most particular friend because they did, after
all, speak to each other whenever they met.

With friends like this, who needs lunch?

The Phantom glides along, Scrooge in tow, to another pair of
businessmen on the street. "He knew these men, also, perfectly. They
were men of business: very wealthy, and of great importance. He had
made a point always of standing well in their esteem: in a business
point of view, that is; strictly in a business point of view."

The essence of these men's conversation is, if possible, less
endearing than the previous.

Man 1: How are you?
Man 2: How are you?
Man 1: Well, Old Scratch has got his own at last, hey?
Man 2: So I am told. Cold, isn't it?
Man 1: Seasonable for Christmas time. You're not a skater, I suppose?
Man 2: No. No. Something else to think of. Good morning!

In summary: "Our friend is dead. It is cold. Do you skate?"

What's striking, though, is the way Man 1 frames the
announcement: "Old Scratch has got his own at last."

Old Scratch, an antique nickname for Satan. This guy has pronounced not only Scrooge's death but his final judgment too. Yes, Scrooge's death. We know it's Scrooge, the members of the Silver-n-Snuff gang know it's Scrooge, the Phantom knows it's Scrooge, the reading audience knows it's Scrooge, every actor who has ever portrayed Scrooge knows it's Scrooge. The one person who doesn't know it's Scrooge?

Scrooge.

Scrooge doesn't recognize the man they're talking about because Scrooge is no longer that man.

Confession: I haven't always been the Bible-teaching veteran of church women's ministry that I am today. I grew up attending church, saying all the right words, doing all the youth group things—until the bonds of home life loosened. I spent much of my college years in places and with people who carried me along on a crashing wave away from God. I kept my Christian friends as distant, safe harbors, but I filled my mind, my words, my hours, my heart, with all manner of things distasteful and unpleasant. The year my first novel, *Ten Thousand Charms*, was published, I received an email from one of those long-forgotten harbor friends. She'd bought my book, read it, loved it, and felt compelled to write to me. You see, she was not at all surprised to learn that I had written and published a novel. I'd always been smart—a good storyteller. Talented. What surprised her was the fact that I'd written a novel for the Christian market. The Allison she knew, the one who took off to go to the bars after the Saturday Night College and Careers Bible Study/Service didn't have the spiritual backing to write a novel with a message of redemption. We'd lost track, moved to different states, pursued different lives. She didn't know that I'd grown up a second time, that I'd reclaimed what I'd been so quick to toss away. Still, what a sobering, crushing moment to come inbox-to-inbox with the willful young woman I'd left behind.

Like me, the Ebenezer Scrooge of Christmas Eve was not ignorant of his sin. He loved his sin. Flaunted it. Reveled in it. He liked the dark and the cold, the meager bowl of soup at the tavern where nobody talked to him. It was a life made to shelter him from abandonment as he had been abandoned. He was the sole mourner at Marley's funeral; he expected no more at his own. But now, that man is dead: not in flesh but in spirit. He is a stranger to Scrooge. Unrecognizable. When he stood before the Spirit of Christmas Present, no longer wanting to be the man that he was—at that moment his perishable being became imperishable. His mortal end replaced with immortality, bringing forth the victorious taunt of salvation: "Where, O death, is your victory? Where, O death, is your sting?" (1 Cor. 15:55). The Phantom is not the Ghost of what Will Be, and he is not the Ghost of what May Be. He is, as the English teacher in me fully embraces, the Ghost of the Mixed Unreal Conditional. The Spirit of What Might Have Happened If.

If Marley hadn't come to Scrooge . . .

If Fred hadn't remained steadfast in his love . . .

If Mrs. Cratchit hadn't raised her drink in a blessing . . .

If Scrooge hadn't looked into the eyes of Ignorance and Want . . .

Then, yes, the odious man destined to have a cheap, ill-attended funeral might have been Scrooge. He alone knows the new man he has become. Well, he and the Ghost of the Mixed Unreal Conditional, but the Ghost isn't talking, and Scrooge's voice is trapped. He has taken his first baby step to separate himself from his old life. He's obedient to the instructions in Ephesians 4:22–24: "To put off your old self, which is being corrupted by its deceitful desires; to be made new in the attitude of your minds; and to put on the new self, created to be like God in true righteousness and holiness."

This is a self that Old Scratch can't touch.

17

Bed Curtains and Sugar Tongs

ur first Christmas together, my husband and I had exactly twelve ornaments—a set of little wooden soldiers purchased at a gas station on the drive home from our honeymoon. We didn't even have a tree, since we were married on December 21 and spent most of the season combining our belongings into one apartment. Our next Christmas, too poor for a tree, we bought a single ornament with money earned from recycled aluminum cans, $1.82, and it is the gaudiest, ugliest clump of blue silk and sequins you can imagine.

We still have that ugly ornament. And we still have the soldiers, though most have at least one broken arm or leg. We now have two trees, because one year we had too much stuff piled too high in the garage to bring down the attic access. Rather than rearrange we went to Walmart and bought a prelit one. My ornaments take up two ginormous plastic bins, and they are subdivided in old shoeboxes:

balls, Santa Clauses, guitars (yes, an entire *box* of guitar-themed ornaments), deer, stars/angels, and kid-made (puzzle-piece wreaths, clothespin Rudolphs, Popsicle-stick snowmen). I have a modest Dickens village, a Nativity scene, a ceramic tree, an Advent calendar, Christmas picture books, and two other ginormous containers of miscellaneous, uncategorizable Christmas stuff.

Like other collectors of precious things, I worry about the fate of these treasures after I die. My mother was smart: she pawned off boxes of stuff early enough to enjoy not having to mess with them. But what if I don't get that chance? What if something horrible happens to me and my ungrateful sons just toss out the star-shaped Santa pillow I bought at a craft show for $5 in 1995? What if they split up the set of stockings with our names stitched in my grandmother's perfect penmanship? What if thirty years' worth of well-intentioned but ultimately unaddressed Christmas cards end up in a recycle bin?

When Old Testament Job was stripped (literally) of all that he had—land, livestock, children—and left with nothing other than a full head of hair, the clothes on his back, and his delightful wife, he claimed:

> Naked I came from my mother's womb,
>   and naked I will depart.
> The LORD gave and the LORD has taken away;
>   may the name of the LORD be praised. (Job 1:21)

In some ways, Scrooge and Job share a narrative. Both were men of wealth. Job has three friends to provide philosophical banter; Scrooge has three guides to provide psychological and spiritual insight. Both were supernaturally chosen to go on a mission of self-reflection and leave a lasting lesson on how one ought to live. That Job was inherently good and Scrooge, well, not is irrelevant. Job lived in a time before a Savior died to reconcile sinners to God. Job might be perfect, but Scrooge is perfected, making the end result the same.

Plus, they both die naked. Well, technically, Scrooge doesn't die naked, that we know, anyway. Somebody thought to dress him in his best night shirt, of which he was promptly divested by one of three scavengers: the charwoman, the laundress, and the undertaker's man (again, three). The trio brings the shirt along with the amassed collection of Scrooge's portable property to Old Joe, a gray-haired rascal who runs a seedy rag-and-bone shop "where iron, old rags, bottles, bones, and greasy offal, were bought." From Scrooge's house, they will add: "a pencil case, a pair of sleeve-buttons, and a brooch of no great value . . . sheets and towels, a little wearing apparel, two old-fashioned silver teaspoons, a pair of sugar-tongs, and a few boots . . . bed-curtains ('You don't mean to say you took 'em down, rings and all, with him lying there?'), blankets ('He isn't likely to take cold without 'em, I dare say')"—and that shirt. All of this is tallied up on Old Joe's blackboard and a pittance paid for all.

Jesus directs us, "Do not store up for yourselves treasures on earth, where moths and vermin destroy, and where thieves break in and steal. But store up for yourselves treasures in heaven, where moths and vermin do not destroy, and where thieves do not break in and steal. For where your treasure is, there your heart will be also" (Matt. 6:19–21). These three scroungers may not be thieves, per se. Scrooge is gone, and unless his nephew, Fred, has a need for a new pair of fancy-pants sugar tongs, none of this will be missed. Scrooge watches the transaction and says, "I see, I see. The case of this unhappy man might be my own. My life tends that way, now."

In the next instant, Scrooge is taken to a dark room to stand at the foot of the bed where the body of this "unhappy man" rests, plundered and bereft, unwatched, unwept, uncared for. A cat scratches at the door, and rats gnaw away beneath the hearthstone. But with all of this, Scrooge hears a voice within himself making its own declaration. Yes, this body is the dominion of death, but of the man himself—the honored head—death has no hold. "It is not that the hand is heavy and will fall down when released; it is not that the heart and pulse are still; but that the hand *was* open, generous, and true; the heart brave, warm, and tender; and the pulse a man's. Strike, Shadow, strike! And see his good deeds springing from the wound, to sow the world with life immortal."

The treasures Scrooge will leave behind are not made of silver or leather or silk. His legacy is the open hand, a life lived from this point with generosity and courage. At least, that will be his legacy, we know, because we've seen the end of the movie. We've seen the credits rolling after Tiny Tim's immortal, final blessing.

But Scrooge has one more stop to make.

18

The Name upon the Stone

nce, when I was a little girl snoopin' around the house at Christmastime, I stumbled across (tucked in the back of my mother's closet, shielded with shoe boxes and empty luggage) a set of Sunshine Family dolls. The Sunshine family was the '70s response to Barbie, trading glitz and fashion for crunchy granola wholesomeness better suited for a communal farm than a Dreamhouse. I don't know if I was doggedly opportunistic or woefully unsupervised, but I know I made several visits to that closet during the weeks before Christmas when I would carefully take the dolls out of their packaging, play awhile, then put them back, resealing the tape. By the time I found them under the tree on Christmas morning, posed around their sensible California-style bungalow, they'd lost all appeal.

Since then, I've always been a stickler for the Christmas surprise. I don't rattle boxes; I hate hints. I like secrets to stay secrets until the bow comes off the box.

Scrooge's journey with the Ghost of Christmas Future has been one of secrets and revelation. Revelation: someone died. Secret: Who?

Revelation: the only emotion felt for this dead man is intense relief on behalf of those who owe him money. Secret: Again, who is he? Revelation: the dead man's things are ripped down, bundled up, and sold for a handful of coins. Secret: Seriously, who is this guy?

Revelation: Tiny Tim Cratchit is dead. And here, nothing is hidden.

Scrooge returns as an unseen spectator in the Cratchit home. In stark contrast to the hustle and bustle of his previous visit, everyone— Mrs. Cratchit and the children—sits quietly. Scrooge hears a phrase of Scripture: "And He took a child, and set him in the midst of them." When Bob Cratchit comes in, he is greeted with more subdued fanfare than the last time when he'd burst through the door with Tiny Tim on his shoulders. This time, he has come not from church but from the churchyard. He tells his wife: "I wish you could have gone. It would have done you good to see how green a place it is. But you'll see it often. I promised him that I would walk there on a Sunday. My little, little child!"

Cratchit weeps bitterly but rallies a bit, telling of a chance meeting with Fred, Scrooge's nephew, who offers condolences, sends best wishes to Bob's good wife, and leaves Bob believing there might be a new job in young Peter's future. It is more kindness and consideration afforded to Bob Cratchit in a single public passing with a near stranger than all of his years in Scrooge's employ.

Scrooge listens to all of this, witnessing the moment the family's mournful tears turn into something like joy as they promise, in the memory of poor Tiny Tim, not to be quarrelsome among each other. They share a round of family kisses. Well, Peter shakes hands like a big boy about to go out into the world and earn his keep.

Just in case the audience isn't getting the point, the author pokes in with an observation: "Spirit of Tiny Tim, thy childish essence was from God."

The juxtaposition of the two deaths—the unmourned wretch and the celebrated child—brings Scrooge to press the Ghost of Christmas Future one more time: "Tell me what man that was whom we saw lying dead." And, one more time, the Spirit refuses to answer. Instead, he leads him on a final mini-journey to Scrooge's place of business, now unrecognizable, to a churchyard, to a graveyard, and finally stopping in front of a single tombstone.

This—this is Scrooge's final moment with the Spirit. With any Spirit.

He asks, "Am *I* the man who lay upon that bed?" The man robbed of his puny possessions? The man not worth the trouble of a catered lunch? The man who might have saved Tiny Tim's life? The man who might have been held in Cratchit's esteem?

The question is not—Will I die? Because, of course, he will die. Psalm 139:16 says that our days are numbered with God before a single one of them comes to be. Scrooge's reclamation doesn't add to his life. Not a bit. It does, however, change the narrative of his legacy.

Scrooge knows—perhaps has always known—Hebrews 9:27: "People are destined to die once, and after that to face judgment." His time with this final Spirit has given him a peek into the temporal judgment he faces: dying alone, unloved. Mocked and maligned. But he knows, too, that there is an eternal judgment. Scrooge wants to expunge his name from the stone not to prevent his death but to stop the course of dying as this man.

"Men's courses will foreshadow certain ends, to which, if persevered in, they must lead. . . . But if the courses be departed from, the ends will change. Say it is thus with what you show me!"

The Spirit says nothing.

"'Why show me this if I am past all hope?' For the first time, the hand appeared to shake."

It seems frustrating, almost cruel, that the Spirit doesn't speak. Doesn't comfort or reassure. Why doesn't he transform into big, cuddly, Christmas-Present Jesus and allow Scrooge to crawl into his lap? Why isn't he soft, baby-like Christmas-Past Jesus, and why doesn't he speak soothingly that all is forgiven? The past erased? Why keep silent? Why say nothing?

Because for Scrooge, as for all of us, the understanding has to come from within. Jesus "was sacrificed once to take away the sins of many" (Heb. 9:28), and that single act stands fixed in time.

Scrooge falls to his knees. "Good Spirit, your nature intercedes for me, and pities me. Assure me that I yet may change these shadows you have shown me, by an altered life!"

And, in its most demonstrative communication since the slight nod, the Spirit's hand trembles. Beckoning invitation. Scrooge clutches it. Manages to hold it for just a bit, but when the Spirit shrinks away and collapses, Scrooge clutches only his own hands in prayer.

19

A Splendid Laugh

Ring out the old, ring in the new,
Ring, happy bells, across the snow:
The year is going, let him go;
Ring out the false, ring in the true.

Alfred Lord Tennyson,
"In Memoriam [Ring Out,
Wild Bells]," 1850

he final chapter, Stave Five, "The End of It," begins with a single exclamation.

"Yes!"

A word of triumph, relief, release. Life. Scrooge is alive in every literal and figurative sense of the word. We haven't seen him truly alive since that moment when, as a child, he lived and breathed with Ali Baba and Robinson Crusoe. This, his story, began with death. He came out of the dark and stormed onto the page with a stiffened gait. He spoke with a grating voice. Think about all the years that passed between being a young boy so hungry for companionship that he kept company with the genie peeking through the windows of his middle-class boarding school and the middle-aged man haunted by the spirits floating outside the window of his cold, sparse room. Think of the sister who fetched him home, the fiancée who was lost to fortune, the nephew shunned every Christmas. Think of how many times Bob Cratchit must have mentioned that he had a sick child. Think of how many times he turned away from an opportunity to help the poor. Think about how long it takes to build a wall of isolation so high that people have already forgotten you by the time you're dead.

Now, imagine that this undeserving man hits the Christmas of middle age (which, let's face it, by Victorian calculations is old), and he gets one more chance. One more chance to swap death for life. One more chance to spark light and warmth into a cold, cold heart. Scrooge had been standing on his own grave and awoke in his own bed. Fully, completely, utterly transformed.

Finally.

It only took one lifetime, plus a retrospective journey through that lifetime, plus a time-stopping, round-the-world journey, plus a skip into a chronologically indefinable future to make it happen.

Still—here it is. Christmas morning, and mere hours have passed.

"Do not forget this one thing, dear friends: With the Lord a day is like a thousand years, and a thousand years are like a day. The Lord is not slow in keeping his promise, as some understand slowness. Instead, he is patient with you, not wishing anyone to perish, but everyone to come to repentance" (2 Pet. 3:8–9).

And Scrooge has reached repentance.

It's a difficult transformation to show on film. In his turn at playing Scrooge, actor Patrick Stewart makes this odd, gasping sound that makes it seem like he's about to cough up a (if he had any) hairball that turns out to be a neglected, rusty laugh—what Dickens describes as "the father of a long, long line of brilliant laughs!" In the 1951 film, the screenwriters choose to let Alistair Sim's Scrooge share this moment with his housekeeper, Mrs. Dilber. He comes off as a madman, terrifying her with his joyful dancing and inexplicable urge to stand on his head until she runs screaming from the room.

Dickens gives us Christmas Morning Scrooge in text that mirrors Christmas Eve Scrooge. He who had been solitary as an oyster is now "as light as a feather." The man who was hard and sharp as flint is now "as happy as an angel." Instead of frightening children, he is "as merry as a school-boy." No longer will he be content with a melancholy dinner at a melancholy tavern, for now he is "as giddy as a drunken man." Then, he reaches the ultimate reversal: "A merry Christmas to everybody!" Only, despite the liberties taken with the classic adaptation, there is no "everybody." Scrooge is alone. Christmas Eve Scrooge would have been driving a stake of holly through his own heart for letting those words pass his lips. Christmas Day Scrooge offers the blessing to himself.

The greatest evidence of Scrooge's redemption? He doesn't even know it's Christmas. He says, "I don't know what day of the month it is! I don't know how long I've been among the Spirits. I don't know anything. I'm quite a baby! Never mind. I don't care. I'd rather be a baby!"

He hasn't simply been redeemed.

Scrooge has been reborn.

The Pharisee Nicodemus, when told that one must be born again in order to enter the kingdom of God, asked Jesus, "How can someone be born when they are old?" (John 3:4). No Bible translation is going to have Jesus tell him that one must be visited by the ghost of his dead friend followed by three spirits serving as literary metaphors for the Christ. He merely repeats himself, with emphasis: "Very truly I tell you, no one can enter the kingdom of God unless they are born of water and the Spirit. Flesh gives birth to flesh, but the Spirit gives birth to spirit. You should not be surprised at my saying, 'You must be born again'"(vv. 5–8). And when Nicodemus presses on, still not understanding—or maybe not wanting to understand—Jesus says, "I have spoken to you of earthly things and you do not believe; how then will you believe if I speak of heavenly things?" (v. 12).

In following Scrooge from Christmas Eve to Christmas Day, from the past, through the present, into the future, from death to life, from a grating voice to splendid laughter, from bah, humbug, to Merry Christmas—we have seen earthly things. The young Ebenezer in the schoolroom was born of water; the old Scrooge clutching his bedpost was born through the guidance of the Spirits.

"Hallo!" Scrooge says to no one in obvious attendance. "Whoop! Hallo here!"

But he doesn't wait long for an answer. Scripture tells us there is joy before the angels of God over one sinner who repents (Luke 15:10). As if in answer to his Whoops! and Hallos! Scrooge hears "churches ringing out the lustiest peals he had ever heard. Clash, clang, hammer, ding, dong, bell. Bell, dong, ding, hammer, clang, clash! Oh, glorious, glorious."

20

The Turkey Big as Me

an we take just a second to recognize the true, unsung hero of *A Christmas Carol*? Yes, the Spirits are important; yes, Scrooge carries the show; yes, Tiny Tim is adorable and Bob Cratchit tugs at our heartstrings. But there is another invisible, faceless entity who receives absolutely no credit for saving the day. Reader, I ask you to consider the noble poulterer.

Think about it. He's had this turkey (the size of a not-so-tiny child) hanging in his window for . . . who knows how many days? (I'm really, really hoping it hasn't been more than two.) To think of the labor that went into preparing that bird. I need a pep talk and motivational video just to reach in and pull out that neatly-tied packet of gizzards from the Butterball nestled nicely on my foil-lined cookie sheet. Imagine wielding a twenty-plus pounder, scalding off the feathers, scooping out the innards (does one "scoop" innards? I honestly don't know), and hoisting it on the hook only to have it ignored by everyone in the neighborhood. Sure, its twin-sized ragamuffin may have been too poor to afford it, but we know the neighborhood is peppered with portly businessmen who could take down such a feast. And still . . . nothing. Until, of course, it's Christmas morning, and the poulterer is sitting down to a lovely Christmas breakfast, or putting on his best church clothes, or spending a cozy morning with Mrs. poulterer and their little poults, when—a pounding on the door, and somebody wants to buy that turkey after all! I've often wondered, *What if he had decided to cut his loss and roast it for his own Christmas dinner?* But, no. Early Christmas morning some kid shows up to buy it with instructions to have it delivered all the way to Camden Town.

This is Scrooge's first act as his new self. Mere hours into his conversion, and he is already doing good works. And if we ever wanted to see the battle of faith versus works whittled down to a moment, this is it. Ebenezer Scrooge was reborn before he had a waking moment as a good man. He renounced his old self, saying, "I am not the man I was!" He fully credits the Spirits of Christmas (the entities of Christ) for this new life he's been granted. He promises that he will honor Christmas in his heart, and knows nothing will be done of his own power but from the work of all three Spirits striving within him.

This morning, he has no tangible proof that any of it happened. He's wearing his nice jammies, his bed curtains are intact, and time has not passed. Not more than a night, anyway, and the giant turkey is still hanging in the window.

"For it is by grace you have been saved, through faith—and this is not from yourselves, it is the gift of God—not by works, so that no one can boast. For we are God's handiwork, created in Christ Jesus to do good works, which God prepared in advance for us to do" (Eph. 2:8–10).

Scrooge knew about that turkey. It had been hanging there, waiting, prepared. Now, it was time to put that bird to good works.

This first act of charity is perfect in every way. It is immediate—even after a lifetime of miserliness, Scrooge doesn't hesitate to reach into his pocket to buy the turkey once he knows it is available. Further, at the first hint of inconvenience (the turkey is too heavy to be walked over to Cratchit's), he takes the extra step to hire a cab. The gesture is specific to Cratchit's immediate need. Yes, Bob Cratchit needs a raise in salary (he'll get that), and Tiny Tim needs to see a doctor (that's all to come too). But today, the family needs a good meal. In the annual ritual of horrific generosity known as the Holiday Food Drive, too many people troll the aisles buying three-for-a-dollar cans of creamed corn and off-brand marshmallows. Even worse? The Spring Food Drive in which food pantries are dumping places for smashed boxes of cornbread stuffing and enormous cans of yams. But Scrooge? He buys the best. He sends it with fanfare. And he does it all with absolute anonymity.

Not to mention, joy: "The chuckle with which he paid for the Turkey, and the chuckle with which he paid for the cab, and the chuckle with which he recompensed the boy, were only to be exceeded by the chuckle with which he sat down breathless in his chair again, and chuckled till he cried."

That is the picture of a man transformed.

Hours before, when asked if he wanted to remain anonymous in his charitable donations, he responded that, no, he wished to remain alone. James 2:17 says that "faith by itself, if it is not accompanied by action, is dead."

"Marley was dead: to begin with."

As was Scrooge, carrying "his own low temperature always about with him."

This turkey brings life to his faith. It connects him to the Cratchits, to the poulterer, to the boy, to the cab driver—more healthy, positive, human interactions in a single morning than he has had all year. What's more, this "Turkey" (Dickens ascribes it an uppercase *T*) completely eradicates the small Christmas goose that was to have been the Cratchits' humble dinner. That meal, with Mrs. Cratchit's reluctant toast, will never happen. The man who was the beneficiary of such undeserved favor no longer lives. Before, Bob Cratchit knew his salary made Mr. Scrooge the founder of the feast, but this feast—this miracle turkey—can only be credited to God.

21

A Great Many Back Payments

In his master's steps he trod
Where the snow lay dented.
Heat was in the very sod
Which the Saint had printed.
Therefore, Christian men, be sure,
Wealth or rank possessing,
Ye who now will bless the poor
Shall yourselves find blessing.

John Mason Neale, "Good King
Wenceslas," 1853

ll philanthropic organizations know we are a soft touch at Christmas. The Salvation Army doesn't employ men and women to dress up like bunnies and ring bells outside of Target in the spring. There are no food drives for hot dogs and chips around the Fourth of July. The children of prisoners need gifts all year round—birthdays, graduations, good report cards—but we don't keep an Angel Tree on permanent display in the foyer. But at Christmas? We're already out-n-about spending way too much money on people we love (and ten times too much on people we don't). There's a good chance those commercial endorphins will direct themselves in a charitable course.

Thus, the visit of the collectors of charity to the offices of Scrooge and Marley the night before. They could not have known they were visiting a man completely devoid of any of the qualities listed in 1 Corinthians 13:13. He was a man of no faith, utterly without hope, and ill-equipped for charity. All modern translations of Scripture, of course, give us the word *love* in place of *charity*. Whatever chance Scrooge had for love had long since been squandered away.

"When I was a child," the passage begins, "I talked like a child, I thought like a child, I reasoned like a child. When I became a man, I put the ways of childhood behind me. For now we see only a reflection as in a mirror; then we shall see face to face. Now I know in part; then I shall know fully, even as I am fully known. And now these three remain: faith, hope and love. But the greatest of these is love" (1 Cor. 13:11–13).

Christmas Eve Scrooge was still essentially a child, living all alone in his rooms the way he had spent Christmas all alone as a boy, but over the course of one night, he was able to put all of that behind him. He saw love in the Cratchits' home, love in Fred's home, love in the tiniest hovels, the sickest of bedsides, and the rollingest cabins at sea. He stood in the midst of it, listening in on conversations, contributing his own silent laughter to the jokes. More than that, he has looked into the faces of the Spirits of Christmas—some more revealing than others—and in return got a hard, unwavering, truthful look at himself.

The Spirits fully know him, knowing exactly where to take him, what to show, what to say.

Scrooge sent the turkey to the Cratchits not as an act of obligation or to assuage his guilt or even out of pity for the poor family. The turkey was more than a gesture; it was a token of Christ-driven love, purchased with joy and delivered with anonymous celebration. It is his first act of generosity but far from his last.

Clean-shaven, with a new spring to his step, our Mr. Scrooge takes to the streets of London on Christmas Day and spies a familiar figure across the street: a portly gentleman, one of two who had visited his office the day before. It would have been perfectly understandable for Scrooge to duck into an alley or jump behind a horse cart to avoid a socially awkward moment. After all, just hours before, Scrooge basically told the man that the world would be a better place if the poor would just . . . die. Instead, Scrooge makes a path straight to him.

"Mr. Scrooge?" the man asks, probably looking around to see if there is a constable in sight.

Scrooge replies, "'Yes. That is my name, and I fear it may not be pleasant to you. Allow me to ask your pardon. And will you have the goodness'—here Scrooge whispered in his ear."

In this gesture, Dickens allows a strong foothold for the new righteousness of Scrooge. He is the same man—still Scrooge, reconciled to the fact that there is an ugliness to his past, yet he does not dwell there. In four successive sentences, he acknowledges his sin, concedes his past wrong-doing, apologizes, and moves to make amends. No excuses, no undue explanations, other than the fact that his donation constitutes a great many back payments. How often do we let the guilt of past failures stop us from stepping up to do what is right? As if an act of generosity will only shine a light on all of those missed opportunities? If anyone had a reason to hesitate, it's

Scrooge. Would they sneer at him? Chastise him? Refuse his gift? Yet, onward, Scrooge! This is to be a new life of forward motion, not mired in regret. Then—he names an amount to be donated in the spirit of Matthew 6:3–4: "When you give to the needy, do not let your left hand know what your right hand is doing, so that your giving may be in secret. Then your Father, who sees what is done in secret, will reward you."

Once, years ago, in one of our super-lean seasons, I came home from church and found a one-hundred-dollar bill in the bottom of my church bag. Someone—during the prayer, or during the twelfth repetition of a praise chorus, or while I was turned around chatting— had slipped it in there. I don't know who (though I suspect), and I don't know why, because we always kept our money problems close to the family dinner table. To the giver, that money might have been anything from a chip to a chunk in their budget. To us, it was groceries for two weeks.

We, the readers, have no idea what amount Scrooge has named. It is forever hidden behind that dash on the page. We know only that it is enough to take the gentleman's breath away. We are the left hand; Scrooge, the gentleman, and God are the right. The numbers have no bearing on us. Our message is in the spirit behind the gift and the method in which it is given. Our gifts—whether dropped in a red bucket, placed in an offering plate, or slipped into somebody's purse when she's not looking—should be unexpectedly generous. Surprising, perhaps, even to ourselves. Our gifts should be freely given, as opposed to being wrenched from our checkbooks through gritted teeth. And, perhaps most counterintuitively, our gifts should be given with gratitude. Scrooge thanks the director of charity fifty times for the opportunity to give.

That's something we don't hear often: thanking someone for taking our money. Still, when blessings are given at the end of the conversation, it is Scrooge who calls out "Bless you!" to the man who has just agreed to take his money.

And to think, all this love, all this giving, all this blessing—and our man hasn't even stepped a single foot in church.

22

He Went to Church

ruth: I did not grow up associating Christmas with church. I grew up in a Christian home, went to church every Sunday (morning and evening) and Wednesday of my life, but all of my Christmas memories are rooted in school-school, not Sunday school. All the Christmas programs and concerts, the parties and events played out in the elementary campus cafeteria with its small stage and inescapable smell of green beans. For Christmas, we always traveled to my grandparents' house in a tiny Wyoming oil camp town where, as far as I knew, there was no church. I must have been in high school, after our family had moved too far away to make the Christmas visit, when the calendar aligned and Christmas fell on a Sunday. It never occurred to me that our family would pick up our Bibles and leave a pile of presents to go and do what we did every week. I know there are churches who meet every Christmas regardless of the day of the week, but—we were Baptists. The only thing we do at midnight is put together things like a Barbie Dreamhouse while the kids are sleeping and eat the cookies left for Santa.

For all the pains that Dickens takes to present to us the truth of Christ, the "reason for the season" if you will, he gives the formality of worship very little attention. Here it is in full: "He went to church."

That's it. Not even the whole of a sentence. In contrast, Dickens devotes an entire paragraph to tell us about Scrooge's morning shave.

Now, it is quite possible that despite his grimness, his dour disposition, his selfishness and greed and overwhelming lack of likability, Scrooge may have been a regular attender of church. He was, after all, a Victorian gentleman, and at the time churchgoing was simply the thing to do. A social obligation as well as a spiritual one. A lifetime of church attendance has taught me that, while most of my fellow congregants are wonderful people, there are others who simply aren't.

Scrooge makes a quick pew stop on Christmas morning, but his true acts of worship happen outside of the structure. "He went to church, and . . ."

Here's a quick grammar lesson from a veteran English teacher: the conjunction *and* joins elements that are essentially equal in weight or importance. Consider this sentence: I decorated the Christmas cookies with frosting and sprinkles. The frosting and sprinkles are equally important to the cookie. Or this one: I went to church on Sunday mornings and Sunday evenings and Wednesday nights. All of those attendances were equally mandatory.

Armed with this insight, consider this: "He went to church, and walked about the streets, and watched the people hurrying to and fro, and patted children on the head, and questioned beggars, and looked down into the kitchens of houses, and up to the windows, and found that everything could yield him pleasure."

Everything Scrooge does outside of church is an act in conjunction with the worship that occurs inside of church. The narrator doesn't say, but we can assume that all of that walking and watching probably included greetings and smiles and shouts of "Hallo" and "Merry Christmas." He's patting children on the head, when just yesterday mothers were gathering children to their skirts at his approach. These are the same streets he trod with the Spirit of Christmas Present, only now Scrooge is visible flesh and blood. Most of all, this brings him pleasure. Before, it was said that he liked "to edge his way along the crowded paths of life, warning all human sympathy to keep its distance." And now he's peeking into windows.

Ephesians 2:19–22 says of the new Christian: "You are no longer foreigners and strangers, but fellow citizens with God's people and also members of his household, built on the foundation of the apostles and prophets, with Christ Jesus himself as the chief cornerstone. In him the whole building is joined together and rises to become a holy temple in the Lord. And in him you too are being built together to become a dwelling in which God lives by his Spirit."

Ebenezer Scrooge: a dwelling place for God.

Chances are, many of these people—the beggars especially— would never have a place in Scrooge's church. The pews of Victorian churches were often populated according to societal standing. Rich people worshiped with the rich; poor with the poor. In his walkabout, Scrooge makes the entire city his church. During his visit, the Ghost of Christmas Present had continually sprinkled the populace with a concoction of Christmas spirit. Here, Scrooge has internalized that very spirit and is spreading it through very mortal means—simple human contact. He had never dreamed that any walk—that anything— could give him so much happiness.

His next stop on his Walk of Joy? His nephew's house. And here we'll see Scrooge's first true act of courage.

23

It Is I,
Your Uncle Scrooge

Previously, on *Christmas Party with Fred and Friends*:

An intimate gathering of twenty friends and family take part in a jovial afternoon of singing, dancing, and parlor games, including blind man's bluff, during which Topper makes a move on Fred's wife's plump sister. Later in the evening, in a lighthearted round of Yes and No, clues such as "a disagreeable animal, a savage animal, an animal that growled and grunted sometimes, and talked sometimes, and lived in London, and walked about the streets . . . and was not a horse, or an ass, or a cow . . . or a dog, or a pig . . ." was finally determined to be Uncle Scrooge! to the delighted laughter of all. The old man, Fred says, has given him much merriment over the years. Because, really, who needs a big-screen TV and a Netflix account when you can gather together, play a little piano, chase a pretty girl, and mock your lonely, old rich uncle?

Still—Scrooge was entertained, was he not? And we can't forget the final send-off as Fred raised his cup of mulled wine and wished his ever-absent uncle a Merry Christmas. It is a noble, generous gesture, considering that doing so the previous day earned him a threat of death by holly.

On this Christmas Day, Scrooge won't be invisible. He won't be blending into the wallpaper or fading into the woodwork. He walks past Fred's door time and time again. For a man who spent the night flying over dark, churning oceans and standing on his own snow-covered grave, Scrooge has a hard time finding the courage to knock on this door. In a dash, he finds the strength, the promise of his new life compelling him: "Ask and it will be given to you; seek and you will find; knock and it will be opened to you. For everyone who asks receives; and the one who seeks finds; and to the one who knocks, the door will be opened" (Luke 11:9–10).

The door opens to reveal a housemaid. A "nice girl! Very." Scrooge says to her, "Is your master at home, my dear?" And when she assures him he is, Scrooge asks, "Where is he, my love?" No doubt this girl—this nice girl—is wondering just who this cracked old man is, and as a measure to protect her master, offers to escort him upstairs, ostensibly away from the dining room where Fred and his guests are gathered. But Scrooge refuses her offer. "'Thank'ee. He knows me,' said Scrooge, with his hand already on the dining-room lock. 'I'll go in here, my dear.'"

He peeks around the corner, and everything is just as it was when his visit went unnoticed. The table is laden with food, the party is gathered around it. His appearance scares Fred's wife, but only because he'd forgotten that she was sitting in the corner behind the door.

Fred cries out, "Why bless my soul! Who's that?"

Scrooge answers, thinking perhaps that Fred doesn't recognize him. He says, "It's I. Your Uncle Scrooge. I have come to dinner. Will you let me in, Fred?"

And this is the moment in all the film adaptations that kills me. The rest of the world can shed their tears for Tiny Tim and his little crutch and the empty seat by the hearth and his little portion of Christmas pudding. This moment, when Scrooge comes face-to-face with the only person in this world who truly loves him, the only person who truly knows him (and loves him anyway)—and he has to ask, "Will you let me in?"

Fred could say no. Understandable, considering how Scrooge has treated him all these years. But, of course, he doesn't.

"Let him in!" says our narrator. "It is a mercy he didn't shake his arm off. He was at home in five minutes. Nothing could be heartier. His niece looked the same. So did Topper when *he* came. So did the plump sister when *she* came. So did everyone when *they* came. Wonderful party, wonderful games, wonderful unanimity, wonderful happiness!"

It's easy to look at all of this wonderful happiness and credit Scrooge's spiritual transformation. After all, isn't it he who found the courage to knock on Fred's door? Didn't he ask for it to be opened? Didn't he seek and find his place in Fred's home? Yes, of course, but Fred has been on the other side of that door, all these years, knocking too.

Christmas Eve:

Knock, knock, knock: "You never came to see me before [I got married]. Why give it as a reason for not coming now? I want nothing from you; why cannot we be friends? Merry Christmas, uncle!"

Christmas Present:

Knock, knock, knock: "I mean to give him the same chance every year, whether he likes it or not, for I pity him. He may rail at Christmas till he dies, but he can't help thinking better of it . . . if he finds me going there, in good temper, year after year."

This Christmas Day:

Knock, knock, knock: "Why bless my soul!"

All these years, Scrooge has done nothing but ignore, mock, and reject his nephew. It has been Fred who knocks, Fred who asks, Fred who seeks—and as a true testament to Christmas—Fred who receives.

24

Tiny Tim,
Who Did Not Die

ur youngest son, Charles, spent his first Christmas in an emergency room. He had a horrible, wet, rasping, wheezing cough, and we feared it might be pneumonia. He was five months old. If you haven't had the chance to see an infant get an X-ray, allow me to set the scene: he was put into a contraption and left dangling in a harness while a camera panned around him. The tech stayed a safe distance away, and I was in another room, watching through a window. Charlie was terrified, wailing, coughing, his face red and cheeks wet with tears. I would have risked any level of radiation poisoning just to grab him up and comfort him. It was the first time I'd ever felt truly helpless as a mother. Still, for all the fear and trauma wrapped up in that day, the entire event now lives in two sentences of family lore:

Remember that Christmas when Charlie was a baby and he had to go to the emergency room?

Yeah, that was awful.

A Christmas Carol is a powerful, theological, convicting tale of what it means to have a life-changing encounter with Christ. It has ghosts and spirits, haunted houses and supernatural adventures. We have the comic romance of Topper and Scrooge's niece's plump sister, the tragic romance of Ebenezer and Belle, and the enduring love of Bob and Mrs. Cratchit. It deals with issues of systemic poverty and socioeconomic imbalance. Yet, with all of this, Tiny Tim steals the show. The average person—those who have never even read the book—can quote exactly two lines: "Bah, humbug!" and "God bless us, every one." Everything in the middle is lost, as if the entire purpose of Scrooge's spiritual reclamation was merely to save that child. The diagnosis of Tiny Tim's ailment is intentionally vague. Malnourished? Yes, as are all the other Cratchit children. They are all hungry, all cold, all poor, all susceptible to dying from an everyday respiratory infection. And yet, our narrator gives us no clue about their temporal fate. Yes, Tiny Tim did not die, but what about the unnamed baby sister? Did she thrive as well?

The key to Tiny Tim's survival is found on December 26, in the final interaction between Ebenezer Scrooge and Bob Cratchit, when the clerk tumbles in a little late from making merry the day before. Scrooge attempts to growl in his old cranky voice to make Bob think that he's in trouble, that he's even fired, maybe. Then, with a leap from his stool and a jab to his waistcoat, Scrooge lets loose with the joke: "And therefore I am about to raise your salary!"

Bob trembles. He thinks about grabbing a ruler and "knocking Scrooge down with it, holding him, and calling to the people in the court for help and a strait-waistcoat." But then, Scrooge says, "A merry Christmas, Bob," with such sincerity that Bob cannot doubt his transformation. Tiny Tim will live because Scrooge will raise Bob's salary and in every way assist the struggling family. It's a straight line of cause and effect: salary = healthcare. Once again, Scrooge's transformation brings immediate action. Faith manifested in works, beginning with an extra scuttle of coal for the office fire.

Scrooge, however, is more than just a financial funnel for the Cratchit family. "He did it all, and infinitely more; and to Tiny Tim, who did *not* die, he was a second father." Tiny Tim, unlike Scrooge, was blessed with a wonderful father. We've no reason to doubt Bob Cratchit gives his son—his family, really—the very best that he can. But he has limits. Imagine how vast Scrooge's resources must seem to the Cratchit children! Scrooge is the source of all they have. Ascribing him a role of "second father" implies a level of investment and interest—concentrated affection and direction. In Bob Cratchit, Tiny Tim has a lifelong example of what a good father should be. Scrooge himself never had that. This benefactor that Scrooge becomes is only possible because he has a new Father too.

"For even if there are so-called gods, whether in heaven or on earth (as indeed there are many 'gods' and many 'lords'), yet for us there is but one God, the Father, from whom all things came and for whom we live; and there is but one Lord, Jesus Christ, through whom all things came and through whom we live" (1 Cor. 8:5–6).

Until his night with the three Spirits, Scrooge had many "gods." Money, of course. His life centered on making and keeping as much as he could. But he also had a sense of worship for his solitude. His loneliness. The coldness of his heart. It's a misreading to say that Scrooge was a miserable person before his transformation. He liked being alone. He'd carefully cultivated walls that were as real as those that surrounded the little boy all alone at school. He celebrated it with cruel remarks meant to ensure his isolation. Scrooge lived through himself.

Now, he lives through his new Father. One who will never abandon him. One with unlimited resources of all good things. One who will take the coldest and deadest of hearts and make it beat with generosity and laughter. Tiny Tim Cratchit needs a second father who can provide what Bob Cratchit cannot. Ebenezer Scrooge needs a heavenly Father who can provide what Scrooge himself cannot. It's a common— almost expected—act of faith to trust God to provide what we need to function and thrive in this world. I know our family has faced times of financial hardship and has watched, believing, for God to provide. We proclaim his ownership of the cattle on a thousand hills, and trust that he'll allow us to have the little bit we need for the next car payment. Or to get us through bouts of unemployment. So, yes, God is an endless resource and generous provider of material needs. But we mustn't forget that he is also an inexhaustible source of those things that make life not only possible but enjoyable. He is our constant font of hope, of joy, of comfort. We can pray to him for healing and also for the strength to endure the hardship. We can ask him to restore a relationship, and depend on him for comfort in the meantime.

The text says, simply, that Tiny Tim did not die. True. But then, neither did Scrooge. While Tiny Tim might be the heart of the story, the little life we want to save, Ebenezer Scrooge is the heart of the reader. The life we want to live. One that can face the hurts of the past and be healed. One that can see the needs of the present and be generous. One that can look boldly into the future and imagine a legacy of goodness. We want to be the one who has an encounter with Christ and is forever changed.

Within the pages of the novel, Tiny Tim has been alive since 1843, and when we turn the last page, he lives on. Just so with Scrooge. Just so with all of us.

25

Keeping Christmas

crooge was better than his word. He did it all, and infinitely more; and to Tiny Tim, who did *not* die, he was a second father. He became as good a friend, as good a master, and as good a man, as the good old city knew."

Scrooge's encounter with the Spirits of Christmas gave him an entirely new life. Where he had no children, he became a father. Where he had no friends, he gained companions. Where he had been feared and reviled, he became beloved and respected. In short, he became what all of us should aspire to be. And he did it through no orchestration of his own.

Why Scrooge? We know there were other odious men in London who could use a good lesson in Christian principles. We can surmise, too, that there were other "good" men who might have just needed a wee bit of a nudge to be "better" men. Why Scrooge instead of someone in power who could actually enact laws to better care for the poor? Why Scrooge instead of a minister who had a knowledge of Christ's teachings and could move an entire congregation to action?

Why Scrooge instead of the poulterer, who should really stock more affordable birds?

For that matter, why Charles Dickens? Why would God choose this man to write an indelible tale of the transformative power of Christ? Dickens was not what you would call a pillar of godliness. He was vain and ambitious, an inattentive father and serial adulterer. He grew up in poverty and had an unflinching distaste for the system that kept people mired there, but he was not known for invoking the name of Christ in his assault. Even in *A Christmas Carol*, his sole concession to what we now call the "reason for the season" is an acknowledgement of the sacred name and origin of Christmas. Evangelical historians can list the names of dozens of other, better-qualified men from the century surrounding Charles Dickens (we have to come into the next century to add women to the list). And yet, nobody's making plans to make a movie based on Jonathan Edwards's sermon: *Muppets in the Hands of an Angry God*.

So, why Scrooge?

Why Dickens?

Because . . . why not?

Because . . . God is sovereign, and he will choose whom he chooses (Rom. 9:15).

[God] has saved us and called us to a holy life—not because of anything we have done but because of his own purpose and grace. This grace was given us in Christ Jesus before the beginning of time, but it has now been revealed through the appearing of our Savior, Christ Jesus, who has destroyed death and has brought life and immortality to light through the gospel. (2 Tim. 1:9–10)

Did Dickens intend for this book to be an illustration of the soul-saving, eternity-ensuring, life-altering experience of salvation through the shed blood of Jesus Christ? Short answer: I don't know. Honest answer: probably not. Would Dickens appreciate this particular collection of writings about his most famous work? Short answer: I don't know. Honest (painful) answer: probably not. But if God can take things that were intended for evil and make them work for good (Gen. 50:20), why can't he take that which is intended for good and make it work for something eternal?

I can imagine Charles Dickens coming across the parable of the rich man and Lazarus—perhaps hearing it from a pompous vicar behind a pulpit. He hears the rich man beg Abraham to send someone from the dead to bring the living to repentance and Abraham's reply: "If they do not listen to Moses and the Prophets, they will not be convinced even if someone rises from the dead" (Luke 16:31).

Picture it: Charles Dickens, staring down at his ink-stained fingers and thinking, *Really? Wouldn't they? Who better to convince a man how to live than a man who has both lived and died?*

If you look around you this Christmas morning, you'll see the trimmings of the holiday. The tree, the stockings, the gifts (the piles of paper ripped from the gifts). At my house we sip coffee and eat monkey bread and watch Ralphie in *A Christmas Story* get his eye shot out for the millionth time. And, if it's a Sunday, we even go to church. All of that is fine for celebrating Christmas, but *keeping* Christmas is something else altogether.

Keeping Christmas is welcoming laughter to a voice too long silent.

Keeping Christmas is treasuring those things that others might deem worthless.

Keeping Christmas is seeking opportunities to do good . . . and then actually doing those things.

Keeping Christmas is forgiving family and asking forgiveness in return.

Keeping Christmas means joining others in worshiping the Savior who saves us.

Keeping Christmas is acknowledging wrongdoing and making amends.

Keeping Christmas happens in the smallest gestures and the largest gifts.

Scrooge was known to be a man who "knew how to keep Christmas well, if any man alive possessed the knowledge." To keep Christmas means to live a good life in this world. To keep Christ promises eternal life in the next one.

"To them [to Dickens, to Scrooge, to me, to you] God has chosen to make known . . . the glorious riches of this mystery, which is Christ in you, the hope of glory" (Col. 1:27).

Christmas in Scrooge, the hope of glory.

Christ in you, the hope of glory.

May the same be said of us, and all of us!

List of Scriptures Referenced

- Reading 1: Dead, to Begin With
  - » Malachi 4:1

- Reading 2: Covetous Old Sinner
  - » 1 Samuel 7:10–12
  - » Ephesians 2:1–5
  - » Ephesians 2:8–9

- Reading 3: Good Afternoon, Gentlemen!
  - » 1 Corinthians 13:13
  - » Matthew 26:35
  - » Mark 14:66–72
  - » Matthew 16:18
  - » Hebrews 10:36

- Reading 4: Air Filled with Phantoms
  - » Luke 16:19–31

- Reading 5: Evergreen and Summer Flowers: Christ in Christmas Past
  - » Colossians 2:8–9
  - » Psalm 103:15

- Reading 6: Home, Dear Brother!
  - » Colossians 1:19–23

- Reading 7: Old Fezziwig
  - » Matthew 6:1–2
  - » Romans 12:2

- Reading 8: Belle, with a Full Heart
  - » Matthew 6:24
  - » Matthew 19:16–22

- Reading 9: The Empty Scabbard: Christ in His Brother
  - » Isaiah 9:6
  - » John 10:10

- Reading 10: A Peculiar Flavor Sprinkled from the Torch
  - » 2 Corinthians 2:14–17

- Reading 11: Bob Cratchit's Dwelling
  - » Psalm 22:26 footnote
  - » Matthew 5:5

- Reading 12: Here Is a New Game
  - » Galatians 6:9
  - » Philippians 2:1–2

- Reading 13: Within the Robe: Ignorance
  - » Matthew 19:14
  - » Ephesians 4:18, 22

- Reading 14: Within the Robe: Want
  - » Psalm 51:3–4
  - » Matthew 25:40

- Reading 15: A Single Hand: Christ Emerges from the Darkness
  - » 2 Corinthians 5:16–17

- Reading 16: One Little Knot of Businessmen
  - » Proverbs 14:20
  - » 1 Corinthians 15:55
  - » Ephesians 4:22–24

- Reading 17: Bed Curtains and Sugar Tongs
  - » Job 1:21
  - » Matthew 6:19–21

- Reading 18: The Name upon the Stone
  - » Psalm 139:16
  - » Hebrews 9:27–28

- Reading 19: A Splendid Laugh
  - » 2 Peter 3:8–9
  - » John 3:4–12
  - » Luke 15:10

- Reading 20: The Turkey Big as Me
  - » Ephesians 2:8–10
  - » James 2:17

- Reading 21: A Great Many Back Payments
  - » 1 Corinthians 13:11–13
  - » Matthew 6:3–4

- Reading 22: He Went to Church
  - » Ephesians 2:19–22

- Reading 23: It Is I, Your Uncle Scrooge
  - » Luke 11:9–10

- Reading 24: Tiny Tim, Who Did Not Die
  - » 1 Corinthians 8:5–6

- Reading 25: Keeping Christmas
  - » Romans 9:15
  - » 2 Timothy 1:9–10
  - » Genesis 50:20
  - » Luke 16:31
  - » Colossians 1:27

Allison Pittman is the bestselling and award-winning author of several novels, including *Stealing Home*, *Loving Luther*, and *The Seamstress*, as well as the nonfiction *Saturdays with Stella*. A four-time Christy Award finalist and two-time RITA finalist, Pittman is the winner of a Carol Award and of the Mentor of the Year Award from American Christian Fiction Writers. A devout bibliophile, Pittman currently teaches English part-time at her church's private Christian school, illuminating the Christian worldview found in all manner of literature, both sacred and secular.